The Graduate School Guide for Nurturing the
WHY of Your Goals and Dreams

GET YOUR HUSTLE BACK IN 90 DAYS...
Vol. 1

By

Aaron Womack, Jr

HOV
PUBLISHING

FAITH WITHOUT HUSTLE IS DEAD

Get your Hustle Back in 90 Days... Vol. 1

Scripture taken from the King James Version. Copyright © 1982 by Thomas Nelson, Inc. Used by permission. All rights reserved.

HOV Publishing a division of HOV, LLC.
www.hovpub.com
hopeofvision@gmail.com

Cover Design: HOV Design Solutions
Editor/Proofreader: Amy Owens for Clarity Communications

Write the Author Aaron Womack Jr. at:
Email: atrainwomackjr@yahoo.com

For more information about special discounts for bulk purchases, please contact atrainwomackjr@yahoo.com

ISBN: 978-1-955107-87-7 Paperback
          978-1-955107-86-0 Hardcase
          978-1-955107-85-3 eBook

10   9   8   7   6   5   4   3   2   1

Printed in the United States of America

Table of Contents

PROLOGUE iv

INTRODUCTION xiii

CHAPTER 1 1
Why Not Fight to the Death?

CHAPTER 2 21
Why Not Be Specific with Your Prayers?

CHAPTER 3 45
Why Not Do It Anyway?

CHAPTER 4 59
Why Not Do It Anyway with Faith?

CHAPTER 4 80
Why Not Work Prayer?

CHAPTER 6 99
Why Wait for a Miracle?

CHAPTER 7 115
Why Sin?

EPILOGUE 131

FAITH JOURNAL 135

Prologue

Don't you hate when people lie? I've been lied to. Someone tried to explain to me that if someone tells you something based on what they believe at the time and it turns out not to be true, then it's not really a lie. Well, I don't care, I've been lied to. It's not that I was looking forward to proving the lie was a lie, or proving the lie was the truth. I couldn't really do that because the only way to prove the lie is a lie or the truth is the truth was to die. The lie I am referring to is that when you die you see a light—a bright light—at the end of a tunnel.

I did not see a light or a tunnel when I believed I died. I didn't want to die to prove true what the movies portray as truth when someone dies. Or as in my case, when someone dies and comes back to life. They often say there is a light; a light either at the end of a tunnel or just a light shining brightly all over the place. You may be asking, "Did you die and come back?" Yes, I did, at least as far as I know. I wanted to go, but I didn't want to go. I didn't see a light, but I felt at peace, I felt calm. I felt like if this is it, then I'm good. However, don't get me wrong, I didn't want to leave this earth on my own accord.

I was scheduled for a routine colonoscopy. I know no one wants to have one but it beats the alternative. My regular doctor referred me to the doctor who was doing the procedure. I don't know, but for a procedure I didn't want to have done, I felt better knowing that the doctor was a female doctor. Not that male doctors don't have the same capabilities, but I was hoping she would be a little gentler than a male, if you know what I mean. Let me state this, there is no such thing as routine when it comes to having any type of surgery, especially considering all the pre-surgical requirements. I not only had to fast for 24 hours, eating only Jell-O, I had to take tablets to ensure my entire insides were cleaned out. I didn't think I needed it because I have a bowel movement every day in the morning, it's like clockwork. After taking the tablets however, I must have still had something left in me.

The pre-surgery was extra tough because I went to work the day before. I have a job where sitting still is not an option. I wear sneakers with my suits because I'm constantly walking and I'm on the go. I stole this idea from women I had seen come to work in their stilettos and switch to their sneakers. Due to the fasting, I was starving and yet couldn't slow down. I wanted to let everyone know that I was preparing for a medical procedure and wasn't feeling myself and I wanted to go home, but I'm not a sympathy-seeking type of person. I had to endure it and make it to the end of the day.

I did make it to the end and was completely worn out. I counted the hours until I needed to take my, let me just call it my empty-everything-out-of-me tablet again. I shouldn't have had much in me as all I had in the last 12 hours was Jell-O. Getting to sleep, regardless of how tired I was, wasn't easy as I hate trying to sleep on an empty stomach. I didn't need a full Thanksgiving-type meal, but even yogurt or a piece of bread would have been better than nothing. There wouldn't be any of that for the night. The next morning, I arrived at the facility where the procedure would take place. I put on the customary ass-hanging-out-the-back, thin, white gown and laid down. A nurse came to take me and informed my wife I would be back in about an hour and a half. Little did I know I wouldn't return for nearly 3 hours.

A few polyps, which could have been cancerous, were discovered. After the anesthesia wore off, I woke up ready to go home. Of course, I couldn't drive, so while I felt groggy, I felt good enough to wait patiently for my wife to stop by the Cracker Barrel to get my stack of pancakes, sausages, eggs, and hash browns; I was ready to throw down no matter how I felt. I couldn't wait to get home and started nibbling on the pancakes. When I arrived home, I couldn't eat like I thought I would. I guess I was more tired than hungry.

I told my wife I was good and that she could go back to work. I was just going to lie down and get some rest. She said she'd lie down as well. I tried to get her to go to work because I didn't need to be fussed over, but she stayed anyway. I laid down for what must have been about 15 minutes and got up to go to the bathroom. I wasn't lying down on my usual side of the bed. This meant as I got up to go to the bathroom in our bedroom, I had to walk around the bed. No problem, only, there WAS a problem. The usual 20 steps looked to be about 200 steps. Boy, I must really be tired. I began to wobble a little bit and grabbed the bedpost at the foot of the bed.

I made it to the other bedpost at the foot of the bed on the side my wife was sleeping; this took a lot of strength. What did the surgery do to me? "Are you alright?" Tosha asked.

"Yeah I'm good."

"You need help?"

"Come on now, I'm good"

But I wasn't good, I just didn't know it. I took a few more steps and fell into the back of the recliner. Just a few more steps to the bathroom, I'm almost there. I remember leaning and holding onto the wall the rest of the way. I remember getting into the bathroom. I remember pushing the door shut. I remember seeing the toilet and thinking I have never been as happy as I am right now in seeing a toilet. I remember starting to untie my sweatpants. What I don't remember was hearing my wife screaming.

I didn't know how long I had been passed out. I woke to hear someone on the phone yelling, telling someone, he's bleeding, and he passed out and he's bleeding all over the place and he hit his head on the toilet! I was trying to see who she was talking about, who's bleeding, who fell, who hit their head on the toilet? I do remember moving and trying to get up as for some reason I was on the floor. I was told to be still, just wait for the ambulance. Why would I wait for the ambulance? Let me get up at least. I tried, but fell. I remember slipping on something slippery, something red, and it was all over the place. It was my own blood. I remember hearing Tosha calling her dad, through her tears, on one phone, yelling to come quick. I heard her say, while on another phone, the paramedics will be here soon. I heard her tell me again to lay down and wait. She told me I fell while trying to get to the bathroom and was bleeding all over. I saw that my pants were half-way down; I must have made it to the toilet and passed out. I told myself I wasn't going to be found on the toilet by strangers, I tried to get up and make it to my recliner. Tosha kept yelling for me to wait. I'm not waiting, too much pride, I guess. I'm not waiting; I'm going into my bedroom. I'm not waiting. My body didn't wait, I passed out again.

This is where I remember that people lied about the light. I remember being in a quiet place, very clear and white, but there wasn't a light. I didn't see the light that people have described seeing when they talk about experiencing death. My mind was at ease and I seemed to be floating along. Not heading for a particular destination, but just floating. I felt relief, that is about the only and best way I could describe what I was feeling or what was taking place. Just relief, I felt nothing, yet that nothingness felt good; I didn't feel like leaving the place where I was. Whatever this feeling was or wherever this place was, I didn't want to leave. I could stay here forever. I would have stayed there forever; except I was being talked to. Talked to by someone, I couldn't tell who it was. I didn't recognize the voice; could it be, might it be Him, the Almighty? I tried to speak but I didn't know who I was speaking to. Was I speaking to a higher being?

I don't know but a voice was speaking to me. I didn't understand what he was saying. I just floated along and tried to understand the voice and what was being said. I closed my eyes real tight to focus, I didn't say anything and then I remember simply saying, "Let me go, let me go." I was ready to go to the place that I thought was heaven. I was ready, nothing could keep me from there, and it was time, until it wasn't time. It wasn't time because I was awakened in the most unusual way.

I was awakened by a slap to my face by a white man in a uniform. He was telling me to wake up, to get up, while he was pulling me up. There were others in my house. How did they get in? There was a lot of talking and poking. I was up and fell back down. I repeated, let me go, I'm good, let me go. The voice kept saying, you've lost a lot of blood, but you're not going out on our watch. Apparently, I wasn't going. Later I found out between the five fire department medics and ambulance drivers, they were going to do everything possible to make sure I wasn't dying on their watch. I wanted to go but they said no. While in the hospital I discovered the doctor who'd performed my colonoscopy hadn't secured one of the polyps and I was bleeding internally.

To make a long story short, I know I died, but I'm back. I could be back for several reasons—it wasn't my time, the Lord had other plans for me, there was other work for me to do. Regardless of the reasons, I'm just glad that strange men decided they were going to do whatever it took to not let me go on their watch. With the amount of blood I lost, my mother-in-law said it looked like a crime scene. She had come over to the house while Tosha and my father-in-law rode to the hospital. My mother-in-law came over to clean up because she didn't want my kids to come home from school and see the blood and not know what was going on.

What was going on was that I had been given another chance. I had been given another chance, in part by five guys who were willing to do whatever it took to help me not see the light, if there ever was a light. They were willing to do what their training had told them to do and what their instincts told them to do as well. Even having to slap me, make me try to stand up, and yell at me. More importantly, this second chance gave me an understanding of the premise of this book. It gave me a Why. A Why for not only wanting to live, but for sharing this story as a motivating means for people to reach their full potential before they actually see the light. The slap came about because I had quit trying to fight to live.

Too often, many don't realize their dreams because they stop fighting. You stop fighting because you don't have a "WHY" to keep fighting or you don't know how to fight. By the end of this book, you will have a reason to keep fighting.

INTRODUCTION

Being able to see a light is not the only lie bestowed upon us. There are several lies that have been imposed on us. Wait, my mom will read this, so I better not say the word lies, but half-truths. But a half-truth is a whole lie. There are several people who have "told a story." This is still lying. I have been lied to and so have you. We've been lied to through our educational systems, from kindergarten to college. We have also been lied to through church and religion. Some people have figured out the lie and have done nothing about it. In fact, they kept facilitating the lie. They pass it down from generation to generation.

But a small percentage of those who figured out the lie and did something about it have gained success in ways that may have seemed unattainable. They have exposed the lie and even have tried to reeducate the masses on the lie and how to get to the truth. Even with the evidence showing what we were taught was a lie, we still came up with excuses as to why certain people were able to overcome the lie and others were not. We even put the truth tellers into a category. We call them the one percenters, among other names. The lie is that we have to wait patiently for our dreams to come true. The one percenters didn't wait, they went after their dreams.

Here is another lie revealed. We were told that success comes through luck. Certain people had a helping hand in society where others did not and that's the only way to be successful. We were told that if it is meant to be, it will be, and that success is about fate. We were told that if we don't have the success or realize the dreams we aspired to, then it must not be in God's will, and therefore we should just appreciate what we have. Is it a sin to want more? Look at those less fortunate than yourself and thank God you're not in their situation.

What is the truth? The truth is that we are responsible in regard to the achievement of our dreams. We must take responsibility. What about faith? If you read your Bible, you know what faith must have, WORK. You must display a work ethic that will take you out of where you are, to where you want to be. Even with busting your ass, there aren't any guarantees. The one percenters have figured out the lie of just waiting for something to happen. To just get that college degree, to just wait on the Lord. Instead, they figured out they needed to go after what they wanted. Yes, some may have done things illegally and have paid the price. But work, work, work, is the truth of having a chance of reaching achievement.

Success can be defined in many ways. Regarding success, Earl Nightingale simply stated, "If you have a goal and you're moving in that direction, you're successful." According to Booker T. Washington, "...success is to be measured not so much by the position that one has reached in life as by the obstacles which he has overcome." Success is not all about material gain. Success, for me, is having a dream in your head and bringing it to life, even if you aren't able to complete it. Mother Teresa certainly had success. Were all her dreams completed? Probably not, however, we are better because of her devotion to humanitarian outreach. All her dreams were certainly not material.

In this book, I want to provide you with some keys to help you maintain the work ethic you will need to reach your goals and dreams. Beyond having a belief in yourself, you need to have something to sustain you for those days you don't feel like working, for those times you want to quit, take a break, or procrastinate. Those days you need a "WHY."

No one, no matter how gifted or talented they are, is immune to wanting to quit at some point. You can do all the planning in the world and have a great game plan, but as Eric Thomas, one of the top motivational speakers in the world, says, life will hit you in the mouth. During those darkest days and times, your Why will get you out of bed, it will have you make one more phone call, it will not allow you to stop at the hundredth "NO." Your WHY may be that you want to make more money, that you want or need a bigger house, that you want to be able to work for yourself.

I will help you on your journey, as the road to success is a journey. In our 3-part series, you will learn 21 Whys I have discovered from studying, not only successful people but success itself. No matter your age, occupation, hopes, or dreams, you can get started right now and set the stage for where you want or need to be. Allow me to share my over 25 years of experience in the education of scholars from middle school to college in the classroom and on the basketball court and help guide you. Even if you don't use the gifts in this book or my other books, seek someone. I have recommended readings for you at the end of each chapter to get the coaching or help we all can benefit from.

The greats, like Tiger Woods, Michael Jordan, Denzel Washington, had mentors or teachers. You will need someone to not only push you but give you powerful insights. There are things you will need to fail at in order to learn, let those lessons lead to not just knowledge, but action. You opening this book is your first action step.

Many people start or even end their day with a motivational quote. I love to read and listen to motivational quotes. I want to leave you with a list of the ones that inspired me the most. To make the best use of this book and to use it as an everyday tool, there are quotes at the end of each chapter. You can read the book from beginning to end and reread it to reflect and take notes. You can also use the quotes to study the chapters one at a time. If I haven't listed the author of the quotes, it is because the author is unknown. Some of the quotes, which are scriptures, often read like quotes for me.

Chapter 1
Why Not Fight to the Death?

"A man is a hero, not because he is braver than anyone else, but because he is brave for ten minutes longer."
-   Ralph Waldo Emerson

"If I were competing on a treadmill, one of two things would happen. Either the person I am competing against would get off the treadmill first, or I would die on it." This is a statement given by the actor/rapper, Will Smith during an interview with Tavis Smiley. The problem is that sometimes life presents challenges to you that don't fit on a treadmill. But the fighting concept is the same whether presented in a neat package or one that is a little messy. Sometimes you have to go to the fight, and sometimes the fight is brought to you.

A fight came to Travis Kauffman on a February morning as he was jogging in a mountain area in Colorado. The Horsetooth Mountain Open Space was an area familiar to him as he had jogged there many times. As he was jogging, the 31-year-old heard a noise. He believed it was just some pine needles rustling on the trail until he noticed a mountain lion chasing him. He simply said he was pretty bummed out. His instincts took over and he did the tactics that the experts said for him to do. He threw his hands up in the air and started shouting. The loud shouts were to try and deter the animal and get it to run off. On this day, what the experts said to do didn't work. You will experience that as well, even if the expert is me. What you're told to do won't work, or it will seem not to work. But what do you do? Do you just quit, sulk, and write me a letter and say that I was wrong? If your WHY is to fight to the death, then you won't even have time for a letter. You may have time for a thought and to say a few cuss words. You may not have time to say a quick prayer. Travis didn't say he cussed at the situation, but he did fight. The mountain lion not only ignored his tactics but then lunged at him. He threw up his hands to protect his face. Whether Travis knew it or not, when wild animals attack, they go for the face in an attempt to get to the throat in order to strangle their victim or prey.

Travis knew to protect his voice and his breath. He was now fighting for his life. When you fight to the death, you encounter two fights. One fight is against the enemy you see, the other fight is against yourself. In the first fight, you work to stay alive, to protect yourself, and to live regardless. The fight against yourself is to keep your spirit alive. We may think we are alive but if our spirit is killed, we are walking zombies. Your WHY is to fight to the death; your WHY is to do whatever possible to stay alive. Protect yourself first, don't die. This is what Travis was doing, protection first, save yourself. One of the rules of airline flying is that in the case of loss of cabin pressure, you should put your mask on first then assist any small child you have with you.

While going for your goals, protect yourself. If someone or something is keeping you from seeing, hearing, speaking, touching, and tasting your dreams, protect yourself. You must live to fight. Kill that spirit or unfriend that person. Once you have protected yourself the fight is not over. It is far from over. The attacker is still there and alive. If the attacker flees, there's still a possibility that it will return. Travis was hoping that the lion would go away. But now that it didn't, in order to win he would have to fight it to the death.

The mountain lion had extended its claws and was scratching his face. The lion was trying to kill Travis. People who try to deter you from your goals and dreams are trying to kill you and will fight till your death or your dream's death. They will put doubt in your mind until you quit. You can't let that happen.

The lions' jaws clamped down to get at his throat. Travis, with his arms up to protect his face, had his arm lodged in the mouth of the lion. Travis fought, he wrapped his legs around the hind legs of the lion to keep from getting scratched or gouged in his private parts. The struggle turned into a wrestling match. The wrestling match caused the fight to roll down a hill.

After rolling down the hill Travis' arm became loose, but his hand was clenched in the lion's mouth. He could feel and hear the tendon in his hands starting to rip and be pulled away. Despite that, the strangest thing to him was how quiet the big cat was. He was shocked by the absence of noise from the cat, no growling or snarling. He thought it would make some sort of noise. When in a real fight or battle, your enemy will not make noise. The fighters that make the loudest noise are the ones you least have to worry about. The true killers, the true killers to your spirit come silently.

The truest killer to your dreams is quiet: the truest killer to your dreams is quiet because the truest killer is you. This is also part of your second fight. Procrastination is quiet, it doesn't shout out "I'M NOT WORKING TODAY!" Fear, self-doubt, laziness, making excuses, are all quiet. They attack you or you allow them to attack you quietly. As I shared in my first book, I am the guiltiest of this. My enemy within kicked my tail quietly. I learned that I can't defeat others without first learning to defeat myself.

Doing battle against yourself is a learning process. I had to learn that everything is not an external enemy. I used to believe that my non-accomplishments were due to outside forces only. When trying to fight outside forces, you may win a few small battles, but the major fights will go down as defeats because you are fighting two against one, the opponent and yourself, all against you. It's hard to defeat you if you don't first understand that you are the enemy. You want to be in a comfort zone. The greats get out of their comfort zone. You must be comfortable being uncomfortable. We all want that extra hour or even extra minute of sleep. We all want that sense of accomplishment, even when nothing has been done. The greats don't relish in receiving participation trophies. Life is indeed a participation sport, but just living does not guarantee a reward. Don't get me wrong, living and being alive is great, but there is no sin in wanting more out of life.

Keep yourself alive by keeping your hopes and dreams alive. Kill off the blockers from within. Then you are ready to fight. Kill off the silent voice telling you what you cannot do and what can't be done.

The lion was eerily silent. But it was attacking, trying to go after Travis' throat. The lion made scratches on his face and body; it had his hand in its mouth, biting down hard. Travis knew he had to do something more. He feared he could bleed to death from the bite marks alone. Travis knew he was in a fight for his life. The lion didn't show signs of stopping or giving up. This would be a fight to the death. Who would get off the treadmill first?

Reaching for his inner Will Smith, Travis began feeling around to try and find any kind of weapon. He grabbed at twigs and branches and began stabbing at the lion. Those didn't work as they just kept breaking. He was desperate, getting tired but not losing faith. He had defeated his natural will to quit so fatigue would not be a silent killer for him. He kept fighting, reaching for a rock he felt by his hand. He started hitting the head of the lion. One blow, two blows, three blows, BAM. I could imagine that if this fight-to-the-death battle was directed like the old Batman television shows there would be big pictures of the BAM and WHAM flashing across the screen with each hit that Travis was giving. But this wasn't T.V., it was real life, and if Travis lost this battle, he would lose his life.

The blows to the head weren't working. The lion was still gnawing at his hand and scratching with his powerful claws. The claws, according to Travis, seemed to be extending and retracting, trying to tear at his intended prey. What could Travis do? The make-shift weapons were not working. He only had use of one arm, how could he keep the lion off his vital organs? He also had to try to keep its claws away from his face and keep his razor-sharp teeth from ripping his arm. He kept hitting it with whatever was in reach of his one arm. The odds were not in his favor, it didn't seem like a matter of if he would die, but how long would it take until he died.

Did Travis Kauffman have a Why to keep him fighting, fighting to stay alive? He had a girlfriend; was she his Why for staying alive? I don't know. After protecting yourself you now must defeat your external opponent. You must fight to the death so that the enemy doesn't get a chance to come back. This is why David, after killing Goliath with his slingshot, went over to the giant and chopped his head off.

Even if the lion released his grip on Travis' arm, Travis didn't know if the lion would try and go after him again. This time the lion might be more successful in getting to his throat and be able to kill him. In his fight to stay alive he now is transitioning to a fight-to-kill mindset. The twigs, branches, and rock didn't deter the mountain lion. It wouldn't quit. Travis didn't have a weapon, what could he do?

Remember what the mountain lion was trying to do to him. Wild animals, animals of prey, try to go for the throat. That's the quickest way to kill their prey by suffocating them. Travis had already tried holding the lion off, it didn't work. He had tried to stab the lion, but it didn't work. He had tried hitting the lion in the head with a rock, but it didn't work. However, he didn't stop working, he continued to do something in the midst of the struggle. That's what you need to do when everything else you tried to do doesn't work; do something. If you want to lose weight but don't know how to work out, and you don't have a personal trainer, do something. Eat a little less and move a little more. Tony Robbins said he is amazed by people who feel frustrated when things don't work for them. He's amazed because they often say, "I tried everything." He says they didn't try everything because if they did, they would be dead. Travis couldn't say, well I tried everything; there is nothing more I can do. There is always something more you can do. He tried one more thing. He somehow was able to get his balance to move his foot and step on the throat of the lion. Once he stepped on its throat, he pressed down on it with all his might.

He attempted to do to the lion what the lion was initially trying to do to him. He was going to strangle the lion. The tables were now turned, even with the tendons in his hand being pulled and torn apart; he found enough strength to succeed because he just DID SOMETHING. If you just do something, you may accidentally fall into the right thing to do. He was weak, tired, losing strength, and unable to call for help, but he found a way. He was talking to himself, pressing down on the lion's neck. He was telling himself that if he could just get some sort of balance or leverage, he could cut off the lion's air by pressing harder on his throat.

In Luke 5:5, Simon told Jesus that they didn't catch any fish; Jesus told them to launch out into the deep. Simon said because the Master told him to do it, he would. In other words, Simon didn't believe Jesus, but he did it anyway. After doing it, their catch was too much for them to take in by themselves. In other words, even if you think doing one more thing won't work, do it anyway. Travis did one more thing.

In order to step on the lion's throat, Travis had to give up the position he was already in, a position he thought was secure. He had wrapped his legs around the hind legs of the lion in an effort to not have it scratch or claw out his private parts. It was a good idea, but staying in that secure position would not give him the victory. How many of you are in a safe place but haven't experienced victory from that position? Why not try something else? Many people won't get the victory they want or deserve because they won't give up the secure position. This secure position comes in many forms, too many forms to mention. But you know what your secure position is. You know what vices you refuse to let go of. You know what your safe environment is.

You even see others let go of their secure position, you see them winning because they took a chance. Could they have failed? Yes, they could have. Could Travis have failed? Yes, he could have. He could have been giving the lion more leverage. He could have been giving the lion the little bit of space it needed to do what it came to do; kill and eat. Remember, Travis is the amateur, the mountain lion is the expert killer, the one born and bred to kill for its food. Although, as Travis would explain later, he didn't think the lion was a full-grown lion, it still had all of the weapons and tools it needed to carry out its mission; its mission was to devour Travis.

Travis took his chance, and it began to work. The feisty mountain lion, after a lot of fighting, scraping, clawing, and biting down on Travis, was growing weaker. The lion didn't have as much fight in him as before. Its air supply was getting less and less. The foot that Travis was using to apply pressure to its neck was working. Doing what the predator was trained to do, going for the jugular, had in effect made Travis the predator.

Unlike the mountain lion, however, Travis didn't have an innate know-how of being a killer. Travis didn't have the luxury of being taught by his parents or a teacher in how to kill. Travis planned that morning how his jog would take place. How many miles to run, what trail to take, what to do if he cramped up. He even knew in the back of his mind what to do if he encountered a wild animal, the experts said to yell and make a loud noise. But this was something new, a fight with a killer with weapons.

Can your plan prepare for everything you will encounter? There are some things life will throw at you that will knock you off your planned day. Some things you have to just take on and win. Some things you will have to fight to the death at the spur of the moment.

Of course, you can't live your whole life just wishing on a hope and a prayer that everything will be alright. You must have a plan for your goals and dreams. I talked about this in Birthing Your Dreams. Remember what Eric Thomas said. "You can plan all you want to and be prepared, but life is going to hit you in the mouth." Life will happen outside of your plans. With his foot on the throat of the mountain lion, the air supply finally did get cut off. The lion, unable to breathe, became weaker and weaker, its movements becoming less and less.

The lion died, Travis was able to release his arm from its mouth, gain his bearings and scramble back up the hill. Even with victory seemingly in his grasp, he couldn't rest. He couldn't rest on his laurels of beating a lion in the wild, at its own game, in its own environment.

Travis explained that he couldn't just rest because he recognized the mountain lion wasn't full grown and he thought that there might be a mother nearby waiting to finish what the young lion had started. There might be another enemy out there. He made it up the hill where other joggers were able to assist him and call for help.

The lion was attacking and fighting because he was hungry and wanted to eat. Travis was attacking and fighting because his hunger was to live. The two were on the treadmill, someone would have to get off first, or someone would die. When life hits you in the face, the gut, the chest, make sure you have a shield of protection, the shield of your WHY. If we're going for the same job and your Why is because you like the job, and my Why is because the job is my purpose, I'm fighting. If we're interested in the same woman and you want to date her, but I want to make her my wife, my Why will keep me fighting.

In this one time event, Travis had a Why to sustain him, to keep him fighting for life. With your WHY, you don't need to have anyone believe or agree with you. When you're fighting for your life, there isn't time for you to take a survey on how many believe you or believe in you. Fighting for your life and fighting to the death is not about a popularity contest. Travis fought to the death literally, but even if you don't fight to the actual death it can feel like the death of something within if you don't at least try. There is no shame in failing, only in quitting.

Recommended Reading:

Built Not Born by Tom Golisano

HUSTLE INSTRUCTIONS
REFLECTION EXPERIENCES

What Did You Learn?

_____

_____

_____

_____

_____

How Can You Apply:

_____

_____

_____

_____

_____

What Is Your Dream?

_____

_____

_____

_____

_____

_____

What Is Your Thoughts?

_____

_____

_____

_____

_____

_____

What Did You Take Away?

_____

_____

_____

_____

_____

What Is Your Goal?

_____

_____

_____

_____

_____

_____

Notes:

_____

_____

_____

_____

_____

_____

_____

_____

_____

_____

_____

_____

_____

_____

_____

_____

_____

_____

_____

_____

_____

_____

_____

_____

_____

_____

_____

_____

_____

_____

_____

_____

_____

_____

_____

_____

_____

_____

_____

_____

_____

_____

FAITH QUOTES
Chapter 1 - Why Not Fight to the Death?

"A man is a hero, not because he is braver than anyone else, but because he is brave for ten minutes longer."

- Ralph Waldo Emerson

"People of mediocre ability sometimes achieve outstanding success because they don't know when to quit. Most people succeed because they are determined to."

- George Allen

"The image of a champion is someone who is bent over drenched in sweat to the point of exhaustion- when no one else is watching."

- Unknown

"Strength does not come from physical capacity. It comes from indomitable will."

- Mahatma Gandhi

"Gold medals aren't really made of gold. They're made of sweat, determination, and a hard-to-find alloy called guts."

- Dan Gable

"The way to get started is to stop talking and begin doing."

- Walt Disney

"Without passion, you don't have energy; without energy, you have nothing."

- Unknown

"The road to success is not straight. It's bumpy, it's hard, it's complicated but, it's worth it."

- Jason Okuma

"We cannot do everything at once, but we can do something at once."

- Calvin Coolidge

"The greats don't relish in participation trophies."

- Aaron Womack, Jr.

Chapter 2

Why Not Be Specific in Your Prayers?

"You don't get rich by doing certain things, you get rich by doing things a certain way."
-   Unknown

"Now she is gone, my heart is yearning
Her love is cold but mine keeps burning
All my eyes could weep but I've gotta keep them dry
Cause the man ain't supposed to cry"

Those are the lyrics to A Man Ain't Supposed to Cry, a song by singer Joe Williams. I was raised with that understanding. I wasn't taught that directly, but it was implied enough by the men in my life. Growing into adulthood I learned that life will throw you a curveball that will make the strongest man cry. In those situations, many will indeed cry, but we will just try to hide it or do it privately. I was faced with a situation where I didn't have time to hide my tears, life threw me a Mariano Rivera type fast ball that had a curve to it.

After a long day of teaching math at Fritsche Middle School in Milwaukee, Wisconsin, I couldn't head home. I was on my way to my class. I was working on receiving a math license as part of my continuing education. You can never learn too much. I made it to class and was working on a problem with my assigned group. I received a text from my wife asking where I was. I reminded her about my class after school. She asked for the location because she needed to talk to me. I asked if it could wait until I got home. She said no and wanted to meet me at my class to talk. I was reluctant to do so. I didn't want to leave the group and the problem we were working on.

Not that the math problem is more valuable than my wife. I have this mindset of people perceiving me as the black athlete and the weak link when it comes to academia. I know, at the age of 42 I was way past my years of playing college ball and after receiving a graduate degree, I should be over those feelings. I'm not, it's what fuels me to make sure I never get outworked by my educational colleagues. "Ok, let me know when you get here."

After texting that she was waiting outside, I apologized to the group, and headed outside. I got in the car and when I saw my wife with that sad look on her face, she began to speak; I interrupted her and said, "so what!"

She said she just received a letter from the doctor. I knew what she was going to say and what the letter was about. She was pregnant with our fifth child. As a blended family we had four children all together and were excited about the fifth addition, only, through ultrasound it might not only be a fifth addition, but a sixth one as well. Her OB/GYN wasn't sure yet, but in the early stages, he thought we might be having twins. My wife was worried about having six kids. How would we handle childcare for two? The expenses, etc. I had heard enough and thought she had come from the doctor with the confirmation that we were having twins.

I didn't want to hear the negative reaction, so I began saying it was going to be alright. I told her that working another job, if needed, was no problem for me. That's why I said, "So what." We have plenty of family members who would be more than willing to help. Plenty of people at church would love to help as well.

As I was talking, she kept trying to cut me off. "But baby."

"But baby nothing. We're fine."

"No, it's just that...." I cut my wife off again.

"It's just nothing; we can handle six, seven, and eight, whatever. Now let me get back to class."

She kept trying to cut me off, but I wasn't having it. I'm a man and I wasn't going to cry over something that could be handled. She stopped trying to get a word in and handed me a letter. It was from the doctor. I kept talking as I opened it, I kept talking, telling her there's no need to cry. I kept talking until I stopped talking. The letter wasn't a letter confirming that we were having twins. The letter wasn't from her OB/GYN. In fact, we discovered later that we weren't having twins. I stopped talking because I started crying.

After a routine check-up, a check-up that was ten years in the making because I hadn't been to the doctor in that long, my doctor had concerns about my Prostate-Specific Antigen (PSA) levels. He referred me to a specialist and the letter from the specialist stated that I had cancer, prostate cancer. We were both crying now. She wanted me to go home with her, but I said no. I had to get back to class. She said I could miss just this one class, but with my mindset, there was no way I was going. I did go with her to put gas in her truck and went back to class.

On my way back to class, I had dried my tears and thought I did a good job of putting my game face back on. When I returned, the group was no longer a group; everyone was taking a break and eating the meal that was catered in. I sat down, not feeling hungry.

"Hey big guy, you not eating?' One of my group members asked.

"No, I'm good."

"We finished the problem. You okay?"

"Yeah, I'm fine, sorry I had to dart out. I'll do the next problem."

"It's all good, you okay?"

"Yeah, I'm fine Astrid," I stated again. I knew she meant well but I just wanted to be left alone. I don't know how I was going to get through the class, but like a stripper, I would fake it. I was trying to block out the noise from people eating and talking and didn't pay attention to Astrid persistently asking if I was okay. I know she meant well, but I wasn't in the mood.

She continued to look at me and said "Something is bothering you." I had tuned her and everyone out. I must have tuned back in because tears began to fall, then I stated I found out I have cancer. Tears came down her face as well, more than mine. It came down enough to where I had to lead her out of the room.

Moving forward there were decisions to be made. The main one was how to treat the cancer and who would be treating it. I decided to have surgery instead of chemo to treat the cancer and had to decide on a surgeon. We narrowed our search to three doctors and interviewed each of them twice. I decided upon a doctor whom my wife said seemed to be a little cocky. While the other two doctors had the same credentials, they talked mainly about what could go wrong. The doctor I chose, Dr. Jacobson, talked about what would go right and how I could have the full recovery I wanted. The full recovery that I wanted was to be able to have an erection.

Yes, while my church was praying for me to come out of surgery alive, I wanted something more. Not just to be alive but to be ALIVE. When I tell this story during speaking engagements, I get some crazy reactions. My premise is that people don't get focused on their specific Why because they don't state to the universe or pray for their specific Why. Successful people do not have a problem with letting themselves, you, their opponents, the universe, or whoever know exactly what they want. Have you ever had a boss who asked you to do something or gave you a task only to let you know what you did was not what they wanted?

Nine times out of ten, they weren't specific enough. You may not be getting what you want or reaching your dreams because you're not specific enough. You may be saying, that's not true, I am very specific in what I want. Let's reflect to determine if you are really being specific. Keep in mind, sometimes, you may not be specific because you may be embarrassed or in the end you don't want to hear "I told you so" if things don't work out. So, reflect, write down not only your dreams but your goals as well. As a reminder from my first book, dreams and goals are not the same thing. A dream is something you want to have; goals are what you do to achieve the dreams. Wrapped around goals are your step-by-step plans to achieve your goals in order to have your dreams. So, pause now to list your dreams and goals.

I can see some of you may be stuck here. If so, then you should have read my first book, just joking. Let me give you an example. I want to be rich. I want to be famous. I want to be a professional basketball player. I stated this years ago when I was a young man. In a later chapter I'll explain how your dreams are tied to you and how you need to work your faith. Many of you probably have said you want to be rich; you may have a dream to be rich. This is not specific.

By not being specific I achieved my dreams, well sort of. I dreamed of being rich and being a professional basketball player. Did I become rich? Not to me, but to others I am. To the homeless person, the person making minimum wage for most of their life, or someone from a Third World Country, I may be rich. Rich is a relative term; what is rich? What about the professional basketball player aspect? I did become a professional basketball player. I played basketball professionally overseas, but not making the type of money I had envisioned. So, I am rich to some but not the rich I wanted. I played professionally but not in the NBA. So, what must you do? These are the three things you must do:

- Believe

- Speak it specifically into existence
- Work your tail off and do it with enthusiasm

Putting it all together; you have to believe in what you specifically speak into existence while working your tail off.

I should have written a specific dream. For example, I want to become a multimillionaire in order to have money as an option for a way out. I dream that I can afford to have my parents' mortgage torn up. I dream I can afford to have a vacation home. My dreams are a want, not who I am. My goal would be who I want to be, or what I will do to accomplish my dreams. I could say by the age of 22—You learned from my first book that you need a due date—I will be drafted into the NBA and be successful enough to have a great 15-year career with an average salary of 15 million dollars a year. Becoming an NBA player would be the goal. The goal would allow me to achieve my dream or dreams.

Again, dreams are not who you are, dreams are what you want to do, or what you want to have. Goals are how you are going to achieve your dreams. If you want to win the lottery, you must buy lottery tickets. Your dreams may be to have a million-dollar home or to retire from your job and the goal would be to win the lottery. Now, you would actually have to buy the lottery ticket first. Of course, winning the lottery is a game of chance but buying the ticket every Wednesday would be your plan. Your daily plans would be to make enough money to buy the lottery ticket.

My daily plan for making the NBA should have been to schedule time to work out every day. When I prayed for an erection, I was specific in what I wanted. Of course, if I am able to have an erection, I must be alive, so I wanted more than to pray to survive the surgery. That is the main reason I chose the doctor that performed the surgery. The other two doctors were good, but when I told them what I wanted to achieve after the surgery, they didn't express much confidence. They told me that only a small percentage of men were able to achieve full erections. Dr. Jacobson, although he did tell me of the risks, displayed an air of confidence in his abilities.

Instead of just telling me of the things that could or would go wrong, he told of the chances that things will go right. He also told me that there are four levels of erections. The levels are from 1-4 with 4 being the highest or hardest, no pun intended. He stated on average, after prostate surgery, most men hover around between the numbers 2-3. I told him I wanted to wait to have the surgery until I was older, and then it wouldn't matter. He said I could wait, or I could be dead. I mentioned to him that the other doctors didn't have his same level of enthusiasm on things being able to go right after the surgery. He said he wasn't like other doctors.

Dr. Jacobson said that the possibility of a full recovery depended on three things: (1) The ability of the doctor, and he said he was the best; (2) My prayer life; and (3) How hard, no pun intended, I was willing to work after the surgery. After the surgery by the best doctor, after praying for an erection, specifically, I had work to do.

I had to reteach myself to urinate again. I wore a catheter then switched to what are basically adult pull ups. According to my doctor it was estimated that I could be wearing the pull ups for up to a year. I had to wear a pull up because I had to potty train myself again; my muscle wasn't strong enough and it certainly wasn't strong enough to sustain an erection. I then made another specific goal, I stated that I would be strong enough to not have to wear a pull up in six months, instead of a year.

I had to get out of the pull ups for two reasons. One, they were expensive, and two, I was attempting to potty train my son at the time. I did several things to try and train him from allowing him to run around naked in the house to putting cheerios in the toilet. This was supposed to make going to the bathroom a game where he wanted to go pee so then he could pretend to shoot down and sink the cheerios in the toilet.

The other thing I was told to do was let him watch me go to the restroom so that he could see what to do. When I did that, I had to tell him that now you have to be a big boy and be able to go to the restroom, just like daddy. I then noticed that when I pulled down my pull ups, he gave me the craziest look, like, how are you going to tell me it's time to get out of my pull ups when you still have a pull up on yourself. I will not be wearing these for more than six months.

Having a skillful surgeon, check. Having a great prayer life, check. Putting in work was next. As I stated earlier, I had to strengthen my muscle. To do this I had to practice what women practice all the time. I had to practice my Kegels. This meant I had to urinate and then cut the flow off. I had to continue to do this to strengthen my muscle. I wanted to go back to work but I didn't want to go back having to wear pull ups. I knew I had to put in work, so I forced myself to work more. To do this I needed to practice more Kegels.

I would drink more water, water all the time even when I didn't want water. This forced me to have to go to the bathroom more often, meaning I could practice the Kegels. When you want to succeed and achieve your goals, you must work more, not just outwork others.

I was now in a place where I didn't have to outwork someone else, I had to outwork myself. In some cases, your opponent is you. If you are an educator, you're not going to the gym to outwork your colleague. You won't necessarily have the luxury of being an athlete and knowing you have to outwork Kobe Bryant or Steph Curry or outwork the CEO of the competing company. So here was my setup.

1. My dream: Having an erection.
2. My goal: To practice Kegels in order to strengthen my muscle.

3. My daily plan: To drink enough water to have to go to the bathroom 12-15 times a day, including 4 times in the middle of the night.

This meant setting an alarm to go off every hour and a half during the night. Setting the alarm was necessary because I didn't want to fall into the comfort zone of just using my adult pull-ups in the middle of the night. This was what I was willing to do. Sometimes during tragedies, you learn certain things that will propel you.

Just practicing Kegels during my regular waking hours, of which was about 8 hours, wasn't enough. I couldn't increase the number of hours in a day, but I could increase my production during the hours. The more I practiced, the more I gave my muscle a chance to strengthen. I specifically wanted an erection, so I did things that focused on achieving that goal. Once you are specific in what it is you want, and the exact dream that you want to achieve, set the goal, establish the plan, and then execute. I was doing my part, so then I could go to God for Him to do his part. What is God's part? My dream—your dream—needs to be big enough that it can only be completed by God. If you can accomplish your dream relying only on yourself, your dream isn't big enough.

Once you are specific in your dreams and goals, once you start to work your tail off in that endeavor, you need to reflect on your plans daily. I write about this in my first book, *Birthing a Dream*. By reflecting, daily, weekly, or bi-weekly, you can determine if you're on the right path or if you need to get readjusted.

Before the use of mini satellites on our phones and cars, my parents would go to a gas station or AAA, to get a written blueprint drawn on a map to show directions to our destination. Exits and on ramps were circled with the trip drawn in a red pen. Even with the map, stops were made at gas stations along the way to not only get gas but to ensure we were still headed in the correct direction. Questions were even asked of the toll booth operator. Part of being told that we were headed in the right direction was also being notified if there were any detours.

There will be detours on your path. How many detours? No one can give you the exact number as they vary depending on who you are and what roadblocks may come your way. Keep in mind that some of the roadblocks will come from you. You will decide to get off the path. There are many reasons for you to make the decision to get off the road to your dreams, from friends deterring you, to procrastination, to you simply changing your mind as to what you want. But all the excuses can be avoided if you make sure to check your passion or enthusiasm. During your reflection, check your excitement for what you're doing.

Keep in mind that nothing great has been accomplished without enthusiasm. You have to have passion or be excited by what you are doing. Not excited for the path necessarily, but excited that knowing the path and the amount of work you're doing is leading you to accomplishing your dreams. Do you think athletes love to workout all the time? Muhammad Ali said he didn't love to run five to six miles at the crack of dawn, but he loved winning. No one can sustain your excitement. There are people who can help motivate you, but your excitement comes from within. Motivational speakers will help push you, but whether you see your favorite speaker live on stage, listen to their CD, watch their YouTube channel, or read their book, those speakers are not coming home to be with you daily. You are going home with you.

Check your passion daily, your excitement daily. I learned about passion during my recovery. As part of my therapy, I was prescribed Cialis and Viagra. Both pills were to have the same desired effect but work differently. Which pill worked better? I'll let you know after I receive an endorsement deal. Cialis was to be taken more frequently; Viagra was to be taken right before I wanted it to work. Not knowing the true use of the pills, I explained to my doctor that I couldn't take either pill as I had planned to go back to coaching boys' basketball. I exclaimed that I couldn't stand in front of my players trying to teach them and then all of a sudden get an erection.

My doctor explained that contrary to popular belief, Cialis and Viagra don't cause an erection. I gave him the craziest look I could give. According to the commercials they do! He said the pills just stimulate blood flow. That's all, that's their job; to stimulate blood flow. The pills help blood flow once you get excited, but the pills don't create the excitement. The Eric Thomas', Les Browns', Brian Tracys', Lisa Nichols', Tony Robbins', Bill Collars' or Aaron Womacks' can't give you passion, they can only stimulate your blood flow. If you're not excited everyday about what you need to do to accomplish your dreams, you might as well go back to your regular job.

Recommended Reading:

"Outliers: The Story of Success" by Malcolm Gladwell

HUSTLE INSTRUCTIONS
REFLECTION EXPERIENCES

What Did You Learn?

_____

_____

_____

_____

_____

How Can You Apply:

_____

_____

_____

_____

_____

What Is Your Dream?

_____

_____

_____

_____

_____

What Is Your Thoughts?

_____

_____

_____

_____

_____

_____

What Did You Take Away?

_____

_____

_____

_____

_____

What Is Your Goal?

_____

_____

_____

_____

_____

Notes:

_____

_____

_____

_____

_____

_____

_____

_____

_____

_____

_____

_____

_____

_____

_____

_____

_____

_____

_____

_____

_____

_____

_____

_____

_____

_____

_____

_____

_____

_____

_____

_____

_____

_____

_____

_____

_____

_____

_____

_____

_____

_____

_____

FAITH QUOTES
Chapter 2 - Why Not Be Specific in Your Prayers?

"You don't get rich by doing certain things, you get rich by doing things a certain way."

- Unknown

"The impossible is often the untried."

- Jim Goodwin

"Always set goals, but never set limits."

- Unknown

"You have to have the mentality of executing your game when you don't feel like there's a lot of hope. I think the best feeling is when somebody pushes you to the limit and you dig down a little bit extra."

- Andre Agassi

"I have never won anything without hard labor and the exercise of my judgment."

- Theodore Roosevelt

"We must all suffer from one of two pains: the pain of discipline or the pain of regret. The difference is discipline weighs ounces while regret weighs tons."

- Jim Rohn

"During critical periods, a leader is not allowed to feel sorry for himself, to be down, to be angry, or to be weak. Leaders must beat back these emotions."

- Mike Krzyzewski

"Winners build on mistakes. Losers dwell on them."

- Unknown

"Outworking yourself means you have to get done what you have to get done. You have to make yourself a priority."

- Aaron Womack, Jr.

"The greatest discovery of our generation is that we can alter our lives by altering our attitudes."

- William James

"Successful people learn to outwork their opponents, the one percenters learn to outwork themselves."
- Aaron Womack, Jr.

Chapter 3

Why Not Do It Anyway?

"If you play it safe, you'll never do anything great."

- *Roone Arledge*

My son attends a pretty good school in Milwaukee, Wisconsin called Milwaukee College Prep. The school has four campuses. My son attends the campus located on 36th Street between Wright Street and Meinecke Avenue. Milwaukee College Prep prides itself on being able to close the achievement gap with black males. They do a good, and as some may say an excellent, job at educating our youth. Two of the campuses, the one my son attends and the 38th Street campuses are very close in proximity to each other. Although there is some great academic work going on inside the schools, they are not located in the best neighborhoods.

To take a tour of the neighborhood you would see the typical boarded up houses, garbage cans at the curb with overflowing trash that has spilled out onto the sidewalks, and abandoned cars. You would see grass not cut, grass that is cut too low, grass that has turned into a place of rest for paper, candy wrappers, empty beer bottles, and grass that doesn't exist. You would see some people out on their porches at six in the morning and those same people in the same spot at noon and later that night. You will see people dressed in the latest fashions walking and talking, walking and talking and again walking and talking with seemingly no place to go. Not being from the area you can be intimidated or scared by what is taking place.

The neighborhood the schools are located in are not detrimental to the education of the students inside the four walls of the schools. In fact, I thought that the students were oblivious to what's going on in the neighborhood until I suggested to my son that he walk from his school on 36th Street to the 38th Street campus. He looked at me as if he had seen a ghost.

My routine is to pick my son up upon dismissal at 3:15 p.m. I then take him back to my school as my day doesn't end until after bus duty around 4:30 p.m. It is volleyball season at his school, and he likes to attend not only to watch his school play but to see his cousin participate. The first two volleyball games started at 4:30 p.m. I usually drive him to the location of the games to watch. The games are played at the nearby 38th Street School. On a Tuesday afternoon, he informed me that the upcoming volleyball game on Thursday would start at 3:50 p.m. This meant that the game would start before I ended my day at my school.

"I can't get you to the game in time, so why don't you just walk to the game?" I said.

The distance from his campus to the other campus is approximately 3 blocks, or 0.3 miles if you go according to Apple maps.

"No daddy, I can't walk."

He could walk out of his building, make a left turn heading north, walk half a block to Wright Street and along 36th Street.

"Why not? It's not supposed to rain or anything on Thursday.

He could then keep going north or turn left to go west on Wright Street towards 37th and then 38th Street.

"Because I'm scared!"

If he goes west, he will make a right turn, going north again on 38th Street one block, although it's a long block to Clarke Street, and then his journey is over.

"Scared of what? Of walking 3 blocks?"

"Yeah, maybe Granny can take me." Granny being his mother's mother.

As I said, the neighborhood is not the best; however, I can't have my 12 year old scared and not use it as a learning tool for him to overcome his fears. Is it a shame to be scared of something? Absolutely not. Our natural fear saves us from danger and can keep us from doing what could be hazardous to our health. But he had to learn that in spite of our fears, we have to step out on that same fear. What is the opposite of bravery? Is it fear? As I stated earlier, it is not fear; it is cowardice.

After I finished my duties that Tuesday, I took him to get something to eat; he brought his favorite pizza and fries from his favorite pizza place, Bricks 3, to the car. Bricks 3 is a New York style pizzeria located within walking distance from my school in downtown Milwaukee. While he was eating, I didn't head directly home. I headed to his school. He must have been too busy eating to even notice that we weren't heading home. He didn't even notice when I made a left turn on Meinecke towards his school. He didn't even notice when I stopped at the corner of 36th and Meinecke, at his school. He didn't even notice when I put the car in park. He didn't notice when I kept staring at him. Then he looked at me, I looked at him, he looked at me, I looked at him, he looked at me again. "Get out," I said. He noticed.

Let me get rid of the ghost he thinks he's seeing. "You said you were scared to walk the few blocks to the other school, so I have to show you what it means to be brave. Walk to the other school. You can take your phone with you."

I didn't notice the laugh or giggle that slowly erupted from his throat as I have never heard it before. I became worried because that laugh was something new to me. I held my ground and said, "Go, I'll meet you at the other school."

After much hesitation, he got out of the car and headed north along 36th Street. I sat in my car and watched him walk the block. It was a long block because I was at the corner and not in the middle of the block where his school sits. I couldn't drive alongside him as he had to walk against the one-way street. I watched him look back at me once, twice, and a third time before he set his sights squarely ahead. He became comfortable with this part of the journey partly because he was walking past the comfort of his school and partly because he was comfortable in thinking I would change my mind and pick him up before the trip was complete. He couldn't have been more wrong.

I left my spot and headed north after my right turn on 37th Street, a one way heading north. I stopped on the corner of 37th and Wright. He had made a left turn on Wright coming west. He smiled at me. His smile broke out to an almost full grin as he got closer and closer to me. I couldn't tell if his smile was genuine or sarcastic. Genuine because it was a relief that his journey was over or sarcastic because he was thinking, I knew you weren't going to make me walk all the way. Whatever the grin or smile was about, it quickly faded when after grabbing for the door handle, I told him to keep walking.

The journey continued west toward 38th Street. I turned left from the right side of the one-way street. Yes, it was illegal, but that's one advantage of driving in the hood. I drove past my son, past the street he would turn right on, 38th Street, as it was a one-way street going south. I drove to 39th Street and disappeared on a right turn heading north on 39th

Street. I must admit, I became a little nervous about what I was doing. I was nervous even when I made it to the destination.

I made it to 39th and Clarke. I turned right on Clarke and glimpsed at the school to my left. I drove back to 38th Street on Clarke and waited on the corner. I waited for a sigh of relief, which only came when my son came into view as he walked on 38th Street. I could see him, about half a block away. I could see him walking past turned over garbage cans, uncut lawns, broken bottles, past grown men with a substance being poured down their throat, and/or another substance dangling off their lips.

He walked past all of that without looking around and stopping. This time when he got to the car he didn't wait to see if he had to actually walk to the front door of the 38th Street campus. He plopped in the seat and ushered a sigh of relief. No smile, or smirk, or giggle. I asked the most stupid of all stupid questions, but I had to have an answer to it. "Was that scary?"

"Yes…It…Was."

"Why?"

"Because I could have been shot or something."

"You could be shot at the mall or at school."

I then asked the question, "What does it mean to be brave?"

He said, "It means being scared and doing it anyway."

Mission accomplished!

The opposite of bravery by definition is cowardice. It is not fear. There are many brave people who are brave while having fear, before, during, and possibly after what they accomplished. Doing something brave is not necessarily evidence of the absence of fear. We all probably would like to believe we would step up on our own in order to overcome our fears and do what needs to be done. The reality is that we sometimes need to have someone tell us to get out of the car. That's what the motivational tapes, speakers, books, or videos come down to. Speakers may do it on a one-time basis while consultants do it on a continuum.

Whatever the case, star athletes, movie stars, and CEOs, have had someone tell them to get out of the car. Some, like Tyler Perry, had to get out of the car he was sleeping in. He went from being homeless to owning a movie studio. Please Google movie studios so you can see the depth and breadth of what he did.

That accomplishment alone deserves its own book or movie.

Take a minute right now to decide what situation you need to get out of the car to accomplish. Whether you're in the driver seat or the passenger seat, whether someone is telling you to get out of the car or if you're telling yourself. Stop reading right now. Put down this book and write down your get-out-of-the-car experience. Write down whether you're driving or in the passenger seat, what street you're on, and describe the surrounding situation. Take as long as you need and then come back to this book. One of my get out-of-the-car situations was writing and publishing my first book. I can't give you all of my get-out-of-the-car situations, as they are too numerous. In fact, all successful people have a get-out-of-the-car situation. Many of them literally have slept in their cars. Also see Steve Harvey's success story.

Recommended Reading: *Soar* by T.D. Jakes

HUSTLE INSTRUCTIONS
REFLECTION EXPERIENCES

What Did You Learn?

_____

_____

_____

_____

_____

How Can You Apply:

_____

_____

_____

_____

_____

What Is Your Dream?

_____

_____

_____

_____

_____

_____

What Is Your Thoughts?

_____

_____

_____

_____

_____

_____

What Did You Take Away?

_____

_____

_____

_____

_____

What Is Your Goal?

_____

_____

_____

_____

_____

Notes:

_____

_____

_____

_____

_____

_____

_____

_____

_____

_____

_____

_____

_____

_____

_____

_____

_____

_____

_____

_____

_____

_____

_____
_____
_____
_____
_____
_____
_____
_____
_____
_____
_____
_____
_____
_____
_____
_____
_____
_____
_____
_____
_____
_____
_____
_____

FAITH QUOTES
Chapter 3 - Why Not Do it Anyway?

"If you play it safe, you'll never do anything great."

- Roone Arledge

"Focus on where you want to go, not on what you fear."

- Tony Robbins

"When you are tough on yourself, life is going to be infinitely easier on you."

- Zig Ziglar

"Few things can help an individual more than to place responsibility on him, and to let him know that you trust him."

- Booker T. Washington

"You'll be surprised how far you can go from the point where you thought it was the end."

- Unknown

"Worry is interest paid on trouble before it comes due."

- William Ralph Inge

Chapter 4

Why Not Do it Anyway with Faith?

Now faith is...
- Hebrews 11:1 (KJV)

The entire scripture is:
Now faith is the substance of things hoped for, the evidence of things not seen.

I can't help you unless you know that in order to reach your lofty goals and dreams, you can't assume that there are guarantees. Just because you work hard doesn't mean you will go pro, become a pro, or millionaire, or accomplish whatever your goals are. I'm here to give you guidance as to what worked and didn't work for me and others, and to let you know that more people have made it through by putting in hard work than those who haven't. More people have made it with a plan than those who simply wake up every day hoping and wishing. Although working hard does not guarantee you will accomplish your goal, be relieved to know that according to Proverbs 14:23 (NIV), *All hard work brings a profit, but mere talk leads only to poverty.*

To get out of the car you need faith. You may say that you have faith, but things have not worked. Please understand that faith cannot be arrogance. The ultimate belief should be in yourself, not in what others believe about you. But you also can't believe at all times that you're the best. Yes, let me say this again. The ultimate belief in yourself is not whether people believe in you but that you believe in yourself. However, don't make the mistake that you are the best at all times. I know this may be contradictory to what others have told you. There may be other life coaches or motivational speakers who have said the opposite. There are some great ones, Eric Thomas, Les Brown, Lisa Nichols, Zig Zigler, John Maxwell, Darren Hardy, I could go on all day. I could list the names of speakers you don't know, people such as Bill Collar. I believe I'm the best because I believe I'm not the best.

Michael Jordan, one of the best players to ever lace them up, became great because he understood there were times, he believed he was not the best. Yes, Michael Jordan. Believing you're the best at all times is an enemy, which leads to others passing you by. How so? Other than being born with unbelievable athletic ability, what separated Jordan? Not just his work ethic, but his Why for working like he did. Michael stated, "I play in games like I'm the best, but I work out like I'm number 2." Oh, my goodness, some of you just missed it. I got excited again just writing it. I got so excited I have to excuse myself and go to the bathroom. I'll be right back.

Ok, I'm back. Successful people keep working hard after their success because during the workout phase, they believe someone else is better. When it's time to compete, then they believe they're the best. You can get into trouble if you always think you're the best. As great as this country is, we have fallen behind in many areas simply because, as a whole, we have thought we were always the greatest. We didn't work out as though we were second best. We have been passed by some educationally, politically, and morally, as well as production wise, and work-ethic wise. At one time in this country it was illegal for people of the opposite race to marry. It was illegal for blacks to go to school with whites. Things are not going to change until this country is willing to get out of the car. To get out of the car you need faith, but you also need the faith to believe that if I'm second best for right now, I can be the best at some point. Excuse the political sidebar, that was just another example.

So, what is faith? One of my mentors, Pastor Claire Atwater simply says faith is "Now." That is why she simply quotes a part of the scripture, "Now faith is." I didn't have my son get out of the car the next day or the next week. Get out of the car now. When you're about to go into battle, your faith needs to be now. You don't have time to have faith for next year, tomorrow, or even in the next hour. Your faith doesn't mean you can't have fear. In fact, do you need faith to do something that doesn't scare you? You can't get a degree in faith, pray for faith, or have it passed down to you. Right now faith, or a lack thereof, can lead you to procrastination. While you need to continue to work to get better, like Jordan said about working as a number 2, when the game starts it doesn't wait for you to get your faith. Whatever mindset Jordan had while working out, it transferred to "right now faith" come game day.

So how do you get "right now faith?" Let's look at the second part of the scripture. I like to use what mega minister from Atlanta by way of Baltimore, Dr.

Jamal Harris Bryant used to describe faith. "Faith is an unshakable belief in spite of circumstances." Combining the two, "Faith is an unshakable belief right now in spite of circumstances." How do you get "right now faith?" Get yourself involved in circumstances that only faith can get you out of. This means not only getting out of the car, but getting back in the car to go to the next destination.

So, you say faith is going beyond your circumstances and doing it right now? Yes. This leads to some great ones even creating circumstances to test their faith. I believe this is why some great athletes make up stories and circumstances just to give themselves an edge, something to fight through. Shaquille O'Neal created the story of David Robinson refusing to give him an autograph when he was a child so that he would have an edge. This was not just to make him thirsty. It created a circumstance to fight through when they met on the basketball court. This is coming from a basketball Hall of Famer.

I had the pleasure of working at one of the top middle schools in the country with high achieving students led by high achieving teachers and administrators. Although I had won a number of awards for my teaching, I had in my mind that I was the low man on the totem pole. I had to make sure my lesson plans were done to perfection. It gave me an edge for my faith to walk in the classroom daily knowing my students would get the best.

Whether you make up this Why, or have natural ones, you must understand for each level, there is another devil. Until you reach the stratosphere area, you won't have to create a circumstance; you have more than enough natural elements to fight through.

Faith does not mean lack of fear, you will never accomplish anything major if you wait until your fear is gone. I know some of you are disputing this right now. In fact, you're probably listing some of your accomplishments that didn't involve you having fear. I am not saying that everything you do must be sprinkled with fear. I am saying nothing major will be accomplished without fear.

The question is not whether fear is a prerequisite for faith. It's also not a question whether fear is a prerequisite for reaching your dreams. The question should be how big are your dreams? Your dreams should contain certain things.

A Major Dream Need to be:

★ So big you can't accomplish it without God;

★ So big people laugh at it;

★ Big enough to get you out of your comfort zone;

★ Big enough to scare you; and

★ Big enough to require faith.

If I say I want to make money, do you think I need any one of those listed 5 items to get that done? Do I need God to make money? Now don't get me wrong, I give God the glory in things I achieve, but I don't go to God in prayer to do the little things. I go to him in prayer to say thank you. You may pray to make, let's say $30,000 a year. I go to him to say $30,000 a day. People don't laugh at $30,000 a year. They will laugh at $30,000 a day.

To achieve that, I can't be in my comfort zone. There are several comfort zones we stay in. Comfort zones of not going for a promotion. Comfort zones of getting a degree you don't have any interest in, but you're expected to do it because of family pressure. By not thinking someone out there is better than you, you stay in the comfort zone of staying popular or being liked, or not having to work harder or going for a higher achievement. If you have the belief that someone is better than you, then you also must believe that you can become better. A way to get better is to work to a point where you experience failure. Failure allows you to get out of your comfort zone.

How can trying to make $30,000 a day be scary? It's scary because in order to achieve something you've never done before; you have to do something you've never done. I have never made $30,000 in one day. As a reminder, this book is not about finding your purpose. This book is about the Why you are doing something to achieve your dreams and goals. I know that I will be of service to others to help them achieve their goals. I have been doing this for a little over two years. That part for me doesn't require faith or fighting through my fears. What I haven't done is service others for pay.

I know my how; I will author books and consult through speaking engagements. That is the comfort zone or in the car zone for me. Stepping out on faith, my get-out-of-the-car experience, is to secure pay for my services. What do I have to step out in faith on and what is my fear? In order for me to become a motivational speaker, I need to have clients. My fear then becomes securing clients.

This involves making calls, sending emails, speaking to anyone and everyone. This requires letting others for whom I've worked on a voluntary basis in the past know that I now charge a fee. This is a fearful experience because some clients might not like me or determine I'm not worthy of the pay. It requires sending manuscripts to publishers, which puts me in a position of being rejected or them telling me that my work is not good enough. I am basically auditioning myself. I can't do that, and you won't be able to either, without unshakable faith. Remember, part of having unshakable faith relies on the amount of work you put in. I must work as if I'm not good enough, regardless of how good my mom says I am, in order to be good enough, then better, then the best.

Why do you need faith? Let's take a look. If you read 2 Corinthians 5:7 (ISV), *For we live by faith, not by sight*, you must live it, breathe it, touch it. If you see that you have something, you don't need faith. This then triggers that if you live by faith, you are alive by faith. If you are alive you can be seen. If you can be seen, then your faith needs to be seen. What, you can't see faith? Luke 5:20 (KJV) states, *And when he saw their faith, he said unto him, "Man, thy sins are forgiven thee.*" Did Jesus really see faith, was it visible and if so, was it visible only to him?

If you read the entire chapter of Luke, you read that a group of guys were taking their friend, who could not walk, to see Jesus. Like many of us do, they arrived late to the house where Jesus was located. The house was full, and they couldn't get in; not even through the window. They climbed onto the roof, tore off the roof and lowered their friend down to Jesus.

What Jesus saw was the action of the man's friends. They lowered their friend down from the roof of a house in order to get to Jesus. This is some faith, tearing up the roof of someone's house. They didn't worry about the consequences. They went into action mode. So, to live by faith you have to display action. You have to be doing something. "Get out of the car, son." I could have asked my son if he believed he had the ability to walk to the 38th Street campus. He would have said yes. There wasn't anything preventing him from having the ability to walk. I could have asked if he was over his fear. He could have said yes. It wouldn't have meant anything until he showed his faith. Yes, faith can be seen. It can be seen not only by Jesus.

I showed my faith in my son first and then he demonstrated his. James 1:6 states, *But when you ask, you must believe and not doubt, because the one who doubts is like a wave of the sea, blown and tossed by the wind.* Don't confuse fear with doubt. If you believe faith is an action, by doing something you have removed doubt, even if you are doing something while being fearful.

I used to believe that when I doubted something I prayed for or doubted my ability to do something, there wasn't a statute of limitation put on that doubt. In other words, doubting that I will ever be financially stable means that I will never be financially stable because I once doubted. Since I doubted it at one time, it will never happen. It is the doubt you had once that may keep you from going forward. But there is a statute of limitations on doubt. Doubt, which comes from lack of faith, which comes from no action, turns into an excuse for not accomplishing goals. Your statute of limitation ends once you put your doubt into action. Faith is seen by your actions. Doubt will then disappear.

In Hebrews 11:6 (NIV) we read, *And without faith it is impossible to please God, because anyone who comes to him must believe that he exists and that he rewards those who earnestly seek him.* Without action it is impossible to please him because your action is your faith revealed. If you don't believe me, take this quick test. Wherever you are, go to a chair. Take a good look at it. Do you believe that the chair can hold you if you sit in it? When is your faith in the chair generated? Yes, when you take action by sitting down on it. What if the chair had three legs or looked visibly broken? Do you have faith that the chair can hold you? You may say no. If you say no, then you have doubts about the chair's ability to hold you. Now let's say you sat in the chair anyway and you were right; the chair collapsed.

You demonstrated your faith in the chair by sitting down. But wait a minute, you may say I still have doubts in the chair, and it was confirmed. Next time when you go to the weak chair, tell God, I don't know how you're going to have this chair hold me, but I know you will make a way. Sit in the chair. This is faith, you acted on your belief. This is action. Do it daily. Do it so much it becomes a habit. Live by faith and then he will see your faith and not the doubt that used to be there but does not exist anymore. John 11:40 (NIV) states,

Then Jesus said, Did I not tell you that if you believe, you will see the glory of God?

You can still have faith that the three-legged chair will hold you. But would you continue to sit in the chair and continue to fall down? Your action of sitting down on the chair should lead you to take other actions; possibly repairing the chair or propping it against something so it will hold you. Now your doubt in the chair turned into action of doing something to make the chair work for you. Your faith turned into action so that you won't continue to fall down.

You have to repeatedly show your faith because you have to be tested to achieve the ultimate goal, perseverance. James 1:3 (NIV) reads, *...because you know that the testing of your faith produces perseverance.* Jesus told me in his word that my faith has healed me, my continued actions, my continued getting out of the car has healed me and allowed me to achieve my goals and healed me of the doubt I had. Bob Iger, President of Disney stated, "The relentless pursuit of perfection is not about being perfect, it's about not accepting mediocrity and perseverance."

Your faith only needs to be the size of a mustard seed. But how does that make sense because what I need is a miracle. If you have faith the size of a mustard seed you can tell a mountain to move. How is it that faith, the small size of a mustard seed, can allow you to tell something as big as a mountain to move? The first reason is that you need to know that your faith doesn't have to be big because your actions don't have to be big; one small step, just moving a little. Just one more phone call, just one more rep in the weight room, just waking up and getting out of bed a half hour earlier than the day before. Just running one mile with an additional 10 steps will lead to the second mile.

You only need faith the size of a mustard seed because of what the seed represents. The mustard seed represents a seed that can be planted. We were born from planted seeds. We grew because that's what seeds do; they grow. We have the capacity to grow in any situation. Mountains are different, they exist. Once a mountain is formed, it doesn't grow. It can get bigger perhaps if snow covers it and then it freezes. But it can't grow.

The mountain in your life, the thing that is preventing you from seeing what's on the other side, can't grow. If you have faith the size of a mustard seed, you can say to this mountain move, and it will move.

Will the mountain actually pick up, hover in the air, and then move to the left or to the right? I don't know and I don't care; I just know that with faith, and getting out of the car, the mountain will move, I will grow to see over the mountain, or I will get the ability to grow and be able to go around the mountain.

Our faith can grow as well. The Bible didn't say we can only HAVE faith the size of a mustard seed, it says we only NEED the faith the size of a mustard seed. In other words, we only need to get started. As I talked about in, *Birthing a Dream*, getting started is one of the hardest things to do. But once we get started, it's harder for us to stop. I don't know about you, but I take comfort in the fact that my mountain, my problems, can't get bigger in my life. Regardless of how big those mountains are, I can outgrow them.

Having faith is not just about believing you can have what you want, it is about self-trust. Self-trust isn't about succeeding; it is about persevering. Every time you fall and get back up, you are building your self-trust. Trust that you're strong, resilient, and that you can do anything you put your mind to.

Recommended Reading:

The Compound Effect by Darren Hardy

HUSTLE INSTRUCTIONS
REFLECTION EXPERIENCES

What Did You Learn?

_____

_____

_____

_____

_____

How Can You Apply:

_____

_____

_____

_____

_____

What Is Your Dream?

_____

_____

_____

_____

_____

_____

What Is Your Thoughts?

_____

_____

_____

_____

_____

_____

What Did You Take Away?

_____

_____

_____

_____

_____

_____

What Is Your Goal?

_____

_____

_____

_____

_____

_____

Notes:

_____

_____

_____

_____

_____

_____

_____

_____

_____

_____

_____

_____

_____

_____

_____

_____

_____

_____

_____

_____

_____

_____

_____

_____

_____

_____

_____

_____

_____

_____

_____

_____

_____

_____

_____

_____

_____

_____

_____

_____

_____

_____

FAITH QUOTES
Chapter 4 - Why Not Do it Anyway with Faith?

Now faith is the substance of things hoped for, the evidence of things not seen.

- Hebrews 11:1 (KJV)

"Unless you attempt to do something beyond what you have already mastered, you'll never grow."

- Les Brown

"If we're growing, we're always going to be out of our comfort zone."

- John Maxwell

"To be successful you have to out work and out faith your lesser foe."

- Aaron Womack, Jr.

"Life begins at the end of your comfort zone."

- Unknown

"If you'll not settle for anything less than your best, you will be amazed by what you can accomplish in your lives."

- Vince Lombardi

"When something bad happens, you have three choices. You can either let it define you, let it destroy you, or you can let it strengthen you."

- Unknown

Chapter 5

Why Not Work Prayer?

*"Nothing can sabotage winning like
the fear of losing."*

- *Mario Cortes*

Having down time from work in the month of June gave me some time to read, do research, and gather information in preparation for this book. It also gave me some time to do things my wife is mostly responsible for during the school year, like cooking and cleaning. I love cooking now, only because I have become pretty good at it and like anyone, I love doing what I'm good at.

I had just completed a 15-day stretch of preparing brats, burgers, baby back ribs, pork chops, pancakes, french toast, sausage, bacon, and a Mississippi style roast. In fact, the roast went over so well that when it was eaten up, or should I say devoured, by two of my kids and a family friend, I quickly made another. From beginning to end it takes about 4 hours to make. Since roasts were on sale for the week, two for the price of one, I had another to prepare. I was tired but happy to have some leftovers on that particular Saturday night. I reminded the kids to be sure not to stay up all night as they had to get up for church in the morning. I told them to be sure to eat so the food could be put away. There were hamburgers and hotdogs left that I had grilled the day before. It was approximately 9 p.m., 8:58 p.m. to be exact.

My kids just stood around. I said we're going to eat the leftovers until they're gone. Still, no movement. I said, "What's wrong, y'all don't like my cooking?" My son said, "Naw, it's good Daddy, but we're tired of bar-b-que." I tried to explain the difference between grilling and bar-b-que to show that we didn't have bar-b-que all the time. I cooked bar-b-que and grilled on separate occasions plus made the Mississippi roast. He said "Yeah, but we haven't had other stuff lately." My daughter said, "Yeah Daddy, we haven't had take-out."

I agreed that there were some things I missed also, like fried rice. When I mentioned fried rice, the kids got joyous and all shouted yeah. I said I could go for some fried rice from our favorite spot, Wings. But as

I checked my phone for the time, I said they're probably closed, it's 8:59 p.m. My son said let me pray that it's open. My other daughter, a recent college graduate, said, "You can't just pray like that." He said, "Why not? I want some rice."

I agreed and said that they're either closed or close to closing and will not take an order this late. I called Wings anyway, more to prove my point. I made the call and was surprised when someone answered the phone. I asked what time they closed for the night. The person on the other end of the phone said that it was closing time as it was 9 p.m. I apologized and said thank you. Then I heard something I wasn't expecting. The lady on the phone was the person I usually talk to as this is the only fried rice location that I frequent. She always recognizes my voice and before I could hang up, she said "Wait, wait! Are you picking up or do you want delivery?" I said, "I would pick up but since you're closed…"

Before I could finish, she asked "Do you want the usual? We'll get something for you."

I said thank you and gave my order. I ran out of the house to get the food. On my return I found my youngest three all bathed and standing in the kitchen with their plates and silverware in hand chanting, "Rice, rice, rice!" They were anticipating the food. As they were eating, my son reminded everyone that we had the rice because he prayed and bragged, "See, I told you it would work."

Did my son get what he prayed for? Yes. Did he get it because he prayed? Or did he get it because I made a phone call to the same place I call every time I want fried rice; a call that is usually made at least three times a month?

I believe in the power of prayer; I believe that God could have snapped his fingers like Thanos and had the rice delivered without my phone call or Wings making an exception for me. However, I also believe part of what makes prayer work is that we must work prayer.

Which came first, the chicken or the egg? Did I make the call because my son prayed or was his prayer answered because I made the phone call? Now, getting the rice is not a big deal; it's not like we would have gone hungry without it. As I stated earlier, we were going to eat the leftovers until they were gone; there wasn't a need to order anything. So why did I even call? What was my Why? Seeing the look on my kids' faces and the cuteness of my son praying, that was Why enough to make the call. But what if the restaurant was closed or they didn't honor my request? How would I explain that sometimes prayers aren't answered? It would have been easier not to make the call. Let me repeat, it would have been easier not to make the call.

On the long and tedious road to success, you will find it will be easier not to do something that you need to do. In studying not just successful people, but people who have achieved their goals above and beyond what they could truly hope for, I learned so many lessons. The one that stood out to me the most is that successful people don't often like having to do the things they have to do to be successful. What do you mean? Don't they love doing tedious work? Don't they love to do the things that others won't do in order to have the things that others won't have? I had a belief that they loved the grind; that they loved to get up at the crack of dawn, stay up late, and make cold calls. Many hate doing those things. Even some great athletes hate putting in the extra work.

Muhammad Ali said that he hated getting up at the crack of dawn in order to run 8-10 miles. Famed

Olympic sprinter Usain Bolt talked about not loving all he has to do in order to stay the best in the world. So why do they do what they hate? The answer is the Why. Successful people have developed a strong enough Why that allows them to do what they don't want or like to do. Muhammad Ali said he loves winning more than he hates running, that is why he runs.

In my first book, *Birthing a Dream,* I took a look at developing a dream from conception to birth. The birthing of your dream, which you treat as your child, happens as a commitment. The birthing of this commitment gives you a Why for doing things you wouldn't have done in the past. Your *Why* doesn't have to be big or elaborate, it can be a small thing like me calling Wings just to see if they were open. But the call was an action, the action wasn't in my prayer, it was in my son's prayer, but his prayer moved me to action.

You must work prayer. As I stated in a previous chapter, there are no guarantees that hard work will get you to your goals, but there is a guarantee according to Proverbs 14:23, which is that all hard work brings a profit. You will profit from the work you are doing. Working your prayer is you simply giving God or the universe something to work with. You can move from a prayer of just asking for things or having those things appear. You can move from prayers to make you rich, make you successful, give you a business, show-you-your-purpose type of prayers. You can move from that to a bless-this-endeavor type of prayer. You can move from a prayer for money to a prayer of blessing what you're doing to make money. Money is important, which I will go into deeper in a later chapter, but you don't have to go chasing it, it will chase you.

You praying and working your prayer is the same concept of a good marriage. I heard Pastor Andre Atwater of Christian Hope Ministry once state, "They say marriage is 50/50. A good marriage is 100/100. Who wants 50% of anything unless it's 50% of Oprah Winfrey's money?"

Just praying without working the prayer is a 50/50 marriage between you and God or you and the universe. I pray and let God do what He does, and then I give 100% as well. Successful people have talents. Each person on this earth has a talent or talents. God is not a respecter of persons. Bill Gates and Oprah Winfrey are not loved more than me, they have just done other things to aid in their success. If we all pray for the same thing, the separation of success is in the amount of work we put into the prayer.

The year was 1994. It was summer, the month of June, not sure of the exact date. One of my former teammates who lives in Milwaukee called me to say he had some tickets to V-100 's Jam for Peace. V-100 is a local radio station here and they were helping to promote a music festival that centers on promoting peace and different people coming together despite their differences. Several singers, comedians, actors, and entertainment personnel landed on the shores of Lake Michigan, in downtown Milwaukee, known as the Summerfest grounds. Of course, I wanted to go, that was a no brainer. In addition to scoring tickets, my friend had backstage passes, which was all the more reason to go.

The entertainers that performed, some 8-10 acts, I can't remember exactly who was there, didn't do a full concert of their songs or of their comedic act. With so many performers there wasn't time. The performers mainly did whatever song they had out that was hot or most popular at the time. For the majority of the acts this wasn't a problem.

The acts started during the day, but the sun was setting over the horizon fast. Different acts were moving in and out of the backstage area, some coming to do their hit and leave, some just hanging around. One of the acts was a comedian who was hosting a part of the show. He was a comedian I had seen before; he was very funny. I liked his act a lot because his main weapon was his ability to rib or crack jokes off the top of his head about anyone in the audience. He was a funny dude who I watched and admired. I was really amazed at how he could come up with jokes so quickly, kind of like a great freestyle rapper who could rap without writing lyrics down first.

I was into comedy because at the time I kind of fashioned myself as a comic. I told jokes and ribbed people in college all the time. In fact, I was talked into entering a comedy contest at Missouri State. Let me tell you, telling jokes and ribbing others in the cafeteria or at football games is way, way, way different than being on stage telling jokes to an audience. The difference is that there is an expectation of you being funny while on stage. I did enter and, of course, I won. Did you think I would mention the contest if I had lost? I still have the plaque, somewhere in the house.

I was encouraged to pursue my comedy but didn't commit fully. I had one other gig. I hosted a Kappa Alpha Psi reunion dinner. I don't remember the jokes I told at either event, but I did practice them for many weeks. So, I know, understand, and admire, the amount of work and skill a comedian must bring to the table. In 1994, I was several years removed from college and hadn't indulged in my comedy in a while. But I always had it in the back of my mind to get restarted. So, when I saw the comedic host of Jam for Peace backstage, I decided to release one of my jokes. With the confidence I had, I didn't worry about being rusty, bombing, or him not appreciating what I was about to do.

Right before I was going to introduce myself and tell him the joke, my subconsciousness pulled me back. It told me I was being stupid, and that the comedian probably has a million people come up to him all the time with jokes. His part of the evening was over, and he might want to just go relax at his hotel. My subconsciousness kept me from approaching him for over 30 minutes. I finally decided to approach him. My decision was based on me dreaming quickly in my mind that he would laugh so hard and be so impressed that he would either take me under his wing and we would hit the road, or he would ask me to be a joke writer for him.

I approached slowly, like a lion in the wilderness approaching its prey. I just didn't know if I was down wind or not. I waited as two other people were standing next to him and talking. I was thinking he's probably bored to death and is hoping for someone like me to interrupt and save him from these two boring fans. They finally left, here's my shot, I introduced myself.

"Hey, how you doing, D.L. Hughley?"

"I'm good, how you doing man?"

"Good, I appreciate you coming all the way to Milwaukee, not many celebrities stop here. They usually turn back to their hometowns after stopping in Chicago."

He said, "No problem, this is for a good cause. But I have to leave to catch my flight."

What should I do? Ask for his number to call him later? Ask how he could hook me up with a gig? I did the only thing I could think of; I told a joke.

"Hey man, before you leave, I kind of dabble in comedy as well, I have this joke I want to tell you."

"Let me hear it."

I couldn't think of one of my jokes, so I told one that I heard from another comedian. I was sure D.L. Hughley had never heard of the joke or the comedian because it came from a comedian who was entertaining at a local comedy club in Milwaukee. The comedian who told the joke wasn't big time, so I was sure I was the only one who had stolen this joke. It wasn't my joke, but I tried to make it mine and would be willing to give credit to the comedian after D.L. hired me.

The joke was about how people complained about Milwaukee, but hey, we should look on the bright side. For instance, we never had to worry about drive-by shootings, because the weather was too cold and snowy. He said, can you imagine a group of thugs, driving slowly down M.L. King Drive, with their windows down, and guns pointed towards their victim. They suddenly shoot and instead of getting away, their tires just spin and spin in the ice and snow. Of course, the key to the joke is the delivery and the sound effect of tires screeching in the snow.

I started laughing hard, but my laughter quickly went away as I saw that he wasn't laughing. He said he had heard that joke before. Dang, so much for my big moment. He then said, "Keep working on your craft, though," and left.

Needless to say, I didn't keep working on my craft. I was going to become a professional basketball player anyway. I left backstage to watch another comedian who obviously *did* work on his craft. I don't believe anyone in the audience knew how much this young comedian would become such a megastar. He had everyone in stitches laughing but who knew what he would become? He would become a megastar of the comedy stage, television, music, and of the big screen. This comedian used to pray for success, but his work matched his prayer life. That's one of the reasons he had success. Unlike me, he was willing to work his prayer. The young comedian was none other than Jamie Foxx.

Recommended Reading:

The Good Wolf by Cedric Boyd

HUSTLE INSTRUCTIONS
REFLECTION EXPERIENCES

What Did You Learn?

_____

_____

_____

_____

_____

How Can You Apply:

_____

_____

_____

_____

_____

What Is Your Dream?

_____

_____

_____

_____

_____

_____

What Is Your Thoughts?

_____

_____

_____

_____

_____

_____

What Did You Take Away?

_____

_____

_____

_____

_____

What Is Your Goal?

_____

_____

_____

_____

_____

_____

Notes:

_____

_____

_____

_____

_____

_____

_____

_____

_____

_____

_____

_____

_____

_____

_____

_____

_____

_____

_____

_____

_____

_____

_____

_____

_____

_____

_____

_____

_____

_____

_____

_____

_____

_____

_____

_____

_____

_____

_____

_____

_____

_____

FAITH QUOTES
Chapter 5 - Why Not Work Prayer?

"Nothing can sabotage winning like the fear of losing."

- Mario Cortes

"Greatness is a lot of small things done well, day after day, and workout after workout, obedience after obedience."

- Ray Lewis

"Dreams and goals don't just come to us; you have to work at them consistently."

- Aaron Womack, Jr.

"When you're tired, sore, and can't do more, that's the time to do more"

- Tim Grover

"When you believe and think 'I can,' you activate your motivation, commitment, confidence, concentration, and excitement - all of which relate directly to achievement."

- Dr. Jerry Lynch

"In terms of instilling the values of mental toughness and work ethic, discipline is the gift that keeps on giving."

- William Baldwin

"The chains of habit are too weak to be felt until they are too strong to be broken."

- Samuel Johnson

Chapter 6

Why Wait for a Miracle?

"If you don't want trouble, you don't want increase."

- *T.D. Jakes*

1 Samuel 17:49-51

Then David reached into his bag, took out a stone and slung it, striking the Philistine on the forehead. The stone sank into his forehead, and he fell face down on the ground. David ran and stood over him. He grabbed the Philistine sword and pulled it from its sheath. And having killed him, he cut off his head with the sword. When the Philistines saw that their hero was dead, they turned and ran.

I was brought up in the church; a Methodist church called St. Matthews. My sisters and I were not just church goers but we were involved in many different aspects of the church. From Sunday School each Sunday to Vacation Bible School each summer. We moved up through the ranks of Sunday School much like a regular grade-school education. There was a ceremony at the end of each Sunday School year. I'm not sure if the church school year coincided with the regular school year, but each year we were ready to move on to the next Sunday School grade. There was even a Sunday School Superintendent, whom I guess kept watch over the Sunday School curriculum, and a Board of Christian Education. This was serious stuff.

We couldn't just attend church and go to Sunday School. We had to join other activities in the church. We started by joining the children's choir. But because we didn't sing every Sunday, if you want to call what I was doing singing, we had to fill in the gap with being on the Usher Board as junior ushers. This meant going to practice on Saturdays, studying the usher's handbook to learn the rules, all while maintaining good grades in our respective school.

I'm not complaining, I learned a lot and it helped shape me as a person through my formative years. I heard a lot of sermons and have been involved in a lot of prayers. Prayers not only at church during so-called church time, but my mom singing and praying around the house. All my aunts and uncles were heavily involved in the church so whenever we visited Chicago or my parents' hometown of Jackson, Tennessee, you better believe we had church clothes packed and ready to go. I learned many valuable lessons from the church through participation and Bible study. I learned that many successful people attribute their success to God or a higher being.

I learned to be persistent, to have faith, to pray, and many other lessons. I studied and valued the examples of the strong men and women from the Bible. Many of the teachings were not just applied to my life but I handed them down to my children's lives as well. To this day, as old as I am, my mom still asks me, "Did you go to church today?" I have been led to a calling of ministering myself. Although I value all of my teachings from the church, I learned one more ingredient that wasn't taught. I learned that you sometimes have to create your own miracles.

Tim Grover began as a personal trainer to one of the greatest athletes and basketball players of all time. He is credited by Michael Jordan for helping to transform him into not only a great player but pushing him into having a great career. A career with six world championships and multiple individual awards. Michael was selected for induction into the Naismith Basketball Hall of Fame. Jordan came into the NBA after having been selected as the third overall pick of the Chicago Bulls. He left college after his junior year at the University of North Carolina.

Tim Grover had a less than stellar playing career at the University of Illinois at Chicago. He wouldn't go on to get drafted to the NBA or any professional league. What he would do was earn a degree in kinesiology and a master's degree in exercise science. He earned those degrees in 1984 and 1986, respectively. Tim wanted to work with athletes to help them perform better. He had formulated his own ideas about the way athletes perform and had his own techniques that could help improve their performance.

During the time that Jordan came into the league in 1984, you would be hard pressed to find anyone in and around Chicago who wasn't caught up in the hurricane that was Michael Jordan. He not only catapulted his own legacy but also that of the Chicago Bulls. Jordan led the league in scoring, led the world in commercials, and made enough money for the shoe company, Nike, that he was given his own signature line of shoes, clothing, and other apparel.

The one thing that Jordan was not able to secure yet was a championship. His team didn't win because of a lack of effort on his part. You know Jordan had to be good because he became the number one problem or enemy of every NBA team. Teams would scheme against him and do whatever possible to keep him from scoring and being successful so that the Bulls wouldn't be successful. Cut off the head and the body would follow; Jordan was most certainly the head of the team. If he played well, the team had a chance to win; if he didn't, the team had…. well I think you know, even if you're not a basketball fan.

If you are a betting man or woman you would more than likely place your bet on Jordan to be successful and overcome the defensive designs of his opponents. To make sure he wasn't successful, one team in particular raised its efforts to make sure Jordan couldn't beat them. That team was the Detroit Pistons. They went above and beyond the call of duty by implementing the "Jordan Rules." They laid a blueprint of attacking Jordan by hitting and beating him as much as possible. They became successful doing this and therefore continued defeating him and his team. The blueprint began to be followed by other teams in the league.

Ending the season with a loss again frustrated Jordan to no end. He wanted so badly to win a championship, just as he had done in college. What could he do? He decided he needed to get stronger in order to take the constant beating his body was enduring. He wanted to get stronger, but he also didn't want to slow down his quickness and athletic abilities. What could he do? He could see the team's trainer and get some advice.

In those days, each team for the most part, employed their own athletic trainer. The team's trainer was primarily responsible for tracking the injuries of the team's players, encouraging them to lift weights, and making sure they were doing their rehabilitation if they needed it. In 1989, after another playoff loss for the Bulls, Jordan was left to spend another off season pondering what he could do to get to the next level. Tim Grover was left pondering the same thing.

How could he get to the next level...the next level of working with athletes to help them improve and to help promote his own abilities? As I stated, during that time, teams didn't hire trainers to work with athletes individually. If a player wanted to work with an individual trainer, like those at a fitness club, they would simply use the team trainer. How could Tim break into the industry? There wasn't a draft for athletic trainers by the NBA. He formulated a plan; a plan that would in effect create a miracle for him.

After attending college and living in Chicago, he knew all about the Bulls and Michael Jordan. The Bulls already had a trainer working for them. How could he break into the industry, the league, and more importantly, the Chicago Bulls? He did what all successful people do, he did *something*. His *something* was to write a personal letter to each player on the Chicago Bulls. Well, almost every player. Traditionally, teams kept 15 players on their roster. Only 12 players were able to be listed for each game. Others were kept for practice purposes and in case of injury. Tim wrote a letter to 14 players.

Yes, there were 15 players on the Chicago Bulls and yes, Tim wrote personal letters to 14 of them. Basically, he introduced himself and shared his desire to be hired by them individually. This was different from the norm, as players didn't have individual trainers. But he knew in order to be successful, he had to do something. His *something* was writing letters to 14 of the players. Why not all 15 players? Tim sent letters to 14 and not 15, because he figured that there wasn't a need to send a letter to the 15th player. He was already the best player, not only in the league, but in the world. Yes, he didn't send a letter to Michael Jordan.

I can't tell you whether Tim prayed that his letters would be answered, that he would be hired, or that he would at the very least get a chance to be the Bulls' new team trainer. What I can tell you is that the 14 players who he sent letters to didn't answer him, not a single one. But he did get a phone call, not from one of the chosen 14, but from the trainer of the Bulls. The phone call was to inform Tim that someone was interested in his service and that they wanted to talk to him. He gave him an address where to meet the person and at what time. A name was not given to him. A name was not listed but what could Tim do? He had no choice but to make the appointment. He made the appointment, rang the doorbell, and was shocked when "The" Michael Jordan opened the door.

He not only opened the door, but he opened the door to Tim's self-imposed miracle. Because he did *something*, he created a miracle, and a miracle situation. How was Jordan seeking him out a miracle? Tim sent letters to every player except Jordan. Jordan, at the time, was seeking to get better, stronger, and improve his overall game. He didn't want to use the team trainer; he wanted his own trainer. He wanted someone who was able to work with him on his personal schedule. He wanted someone as relentless as him. He wanted someone who was as committed and dedicated as he was. He wanted Tim Grover. After their initial meeting, Jordan simply told him to keep up with his pace and rigor.

Tim would go on to work with the *who's who* list of athletes, including Dwayne Wade and the late great Kobe Bryant. According to Webster's Dictionary and a Google search, there are several definitions of a miracle:

1. A surprising and welcome event that is not explicable by nature or scientific laws and is therefore considered to be the work of a divine agency.
2. A highly improbable or extraordinary event, development, or accomplishment that brings very welcome consequences.

3. An amazing product or achievement, or an outstanding example of something.

You are the 3rd definition. *You* are an amazing product and achievement. You must put the work in and let yourself become the miracle. Become a miracle where you receive what others won't get because they are not willing to put in the same amount of work. Tyler Perry went from sleeping in his car to owning his own movie studio. He became an overnight miracle after 8 years of writing plays that no one attended. Go to your phone or computer and do research on at least 10 people you consider to be highly successful or achievers. Do a little more research and you will find that they created their own miracles by doing something. Their something was blessed by a higher being.

What you want to do is have something specific to be blessed. Now, remember, God doesn't bless any mess. However, what you want blessed is the work you're doing, the product you created, or whatever your goals are. Get out of the mindset that you want God to bless you. He has already blessed you. The fact that you are here and alive shows that you're blessed. Be specific in what you want blessed. Do the work towards that blessing. If you want to do well on a test in school, you must study. Yes, you can be blessed to receive an "A," I believe in the power of miracles, but you are a walking achievement and need to recognize that. Ask to be blessed with time to study, ask to be blessed with time to talk with your teacher, ask to be blessed with time to rest.

Your miracle is the work you're willing to do. As motivational philosopher Jim Rohn says, "You can't hire someone else to do your push-ups for you. You have to do them yourself." You can't expect others to work on your goals at a higher level than what you are willing to do. You are the litmus test; you are the higher bar. Do the work and go create your own miracle.

Recommended Reading:

The Alchemist by Paulo Coelho

HUSTLE INSTRUCTIONS
REFLECTION EXPERIENCES

What Did You Learn?

_____

_____

_____

_____

_____

How Can You Apply:

_____

_____

_____

_____

_____

What Is Your Dream?

_____

_____

_____

_____

_____

What Is Your Thoughts?

_____

_____

_____

_____

_____

_____

What Did You Take Away?

_____

_____

_____

_____

_____

_____

What Is Your Goal?

_____

_____

_____

_____

_____

_____

Notes:

_____

_____

_____

_____

_____

_____

_____

_____

_____

_____

_____

_____

_____

_____

_____

_____

_____

_____

_____

_____

_____
_____
_____
_____
_____
_____
_____
_____
_____
_____
_____
_____
_____
_____
_____
_____
_____
_____
_____
_____
_____

FAITH QUOTES
Chapter 6 - Why Wait for a Miracle?

"If you don't want trouble, you don't want increase."

- T.D. Jakes

"Once you say you're going to settle for second, that's what happens to you in life."

- John F. Kennedy

"I don't do things half-heartedly. I know if I do, I can expect half-hearted results."

- Michael Jordan

"Good teams communicate, but great teams connect."

- Unknown

"What you do today can improve all your tomorrows."

- Ralph Marston

"No is a lecture away from becoming great."

- John Hegelmeyer

"I think everyone can be better than they think they can be, and I don't let them dictate that—I dictate that."

- Bob Hurley

Chapter 7

Why Sin?

"We are judged by what we finish, not what we start."

-   Unknown

All have sinned and fallen short of the glory of God (Romans 3:23 NIV). In reading this scripture I am drawn to the word *all*. All means all; not some, not a few, not every other, but all. That means you as well. I have sinned. There, I admitted it; confession is good for the soul, so they say. Whether you confess in person, in a booth, over the phone, or in a letter, confession can help you move on from where you sinned. The Bible says to make a humble confession. I confess, like all other successful people at some point, I have sinned. I have sinned by cheating— cheating on my gifts.

My God-given ability, or abilities, were meant for me. I don't have the ability to sing like I want to, that just means I won't have a dream to cut a record deal. I don't have the ability that Michael Jordan has, that just means I won't go down as the greatest basketball player of all time. I sinned, as you have or will have, by not using my God-given ability and not working hard when given the opportunity that was presented to me. For me, this book was from God.

Take the time right now to reflect on what you have sinned against or how you sinned. What is something that you should have accomplished or completed by now? What great gift was given to you to use for the benefit of others? It may be something given to you by the universe. By not operating in your gifts, you are sinning.

Growing up I had dreams, at least I thought I did, but now I realize that those were mainly just thoughts. They were mere thoughts of making it to the NBA because with a dream, a plan must be put in place and crazy extra hard work must be done. As I shared in my first book, *Birthing a Dream,* and previously in this book, I played basketball, but I never consistently worked hard at it.

I had some talent but routinely made teams based on my height. In 7th and 8th grades I never came off the bench unless we were winning by a lot. My freshman year in high school saw me getting some playing time on the Freshmen team. I was playing on talent alone with no extra work beyond practice. My sophomore and junior years saw me once again not playing on the varsity team. I made varsity my senior year, but I stayed on the bench except for a little playing time here and there. Even when another player on the team, Roger Ruffin, continually begged for me to be put in a game, the coach, after finally having enough, told Roger when he asked why I wasn't getting in, said, "Because I want to win."

I was committing a sin because I prayed for a basketball scholarship and didn't take advantage of the chance to get one by not working hard. God had blessed me with talent; I had faith, but no work ethic. This made my faith dead. Then something clicked in me and I began working out at home and the local YMCA. I did push-ups, lifted weights, and began strengthening my left leg which had weakened from a knee operation in 7th grade. One of my teammates noticed I was getting stronger; maybe my work was paying off.

I finally received some playing time and even started against our rival, the Nicolet Knights, due to another player's injuries. With my new work ethic, I began to make some noise and felt better about my captain status. Yes, I was voted captain even though at the start of the season I was a scrub. I ended the year in the starting lineup and in our final game I led the team in scoring in the sectional semifinals.

With the season over, and no scholarship opportunities, as I stated before I signed up for the Army Reserve in order to pay for college. I didn't want to go but what choice did I have? A choice did come through the law of attraction or God answering my prayers. A college coach saw me play and called to recruit me. It wasn't at a Division I school, it was a Division II school, the University of Wisconsin - Parkside. The assistant coach who called me said he came to see another player play, but he liked what he saw in that when I played, I played hard and never stopped running. During the last half of my senior year, even before I became a starter in the last three games, I told myself I was going to give my all for the three, then five, then ten, then fifteen minutes of playing time. Since I matched faith with working hard, I had stopped sinning.

I began to understand that God gives us everything we need to be successful. The one thing that He doesn't give us is faith; therefore, he doesn't give us work. We must supply that ourselves. He has faith in us, but we must work hard, which shows our faith. Think about it, I didn't work hard because I didn't have the faith that my hard work would pay off. Is that why you haven't put as much effort into your dream? You lack the faith to believe you can actually achieve what you want? You may have put in work but have not seen the results you wanted in the time you wanted, so you quit. Maybe not quit altogether but you lowered your work ethic. You no longer get up early or stay up late. You read less or stop going to seminars. When you lower your work ethic, you lower your faith.

If you ask God to move a mountain, you better be ready to wake up next to a shovel. Although you only need faith the size of a mustard seed in order to speak to a mountain and tell it to move, you need the work ethic of the entire mountain to get it to move in the direction you want it to go.

By not working hard, which leads to not having faith, it signifies that you don't believe, which is the sin. I stopped sinning, in other words, I started working hard, and received a scholarship. But I started sinning again by not working as hard as I did previously. After receiving the scholarship, I realized that I wasn't the number one recruit. There were other players on the team, some with more talent and all with a better work ethic. I went back to being at the bottom of the barrel. I was considered a project and was redshirted. This meant I practiced with the team but didn't play in games. Not having games to look forward to and not understanding I needed to work even harder sent me back to sinning.

Once you stop sinning by putting in work, you can still go back to sinning. The work ethic needed to get you to one level is not necessarily the one that will maintain you. Elon Musk has an incredible work ethic, and he certainly has faith, unwavering faith. He was successful with his PayPal venture and made a mountain of money when he sold it. As an engineer he stepped out of his comfort zone by creating a car company. He was entering a field in which all the major car companies had an almost 80-year head start and advantage over him. He had some failures and was close to losing his company. But what did he do? He showed his faith by working harder. He went almost sleepless for weeks in an attempt to turn his Tesla car company into one that is profitable.

The successful may have sinned previously, but they recognize their sins early, make the adjustments, and stay away from sin. They can out-faith their lesser foes. This work ethic will reward you. Whether through the law of attraction or your faith matching what God has for you, your reward will come your way. Even when you return to sinning, you can pull yourself back up. This is what happened to me.

After my freshman year at UW-Parkside, I knew I didn't work hard during the previous season. I worked just hard enough to make it through practice, but not hard enough to improve. I spent the summer after my freshman season putting in work. I lifted weights and changed my diet.

God has faith in us because he gave us the ability. But he doesn't give us faith in ourselves; we have to do that through our work ethic. He has faith in us because he made us. I know this may be a hard concept to accept, but without working hard to match your gifts, you are operating below what you were intended to do. By underutilizing your gifts because you are working below what you are capable of, you turn your gifts into a sin.

Dreams and goals are like God, they are jealous. If you don't pay attention to them or if you ignore them for too long, they can attach themselves to someone else. They don't necessarily come to us. We must work for them. We must go after them and pursue them. While pursuing them, you don't have to wait to get all of the skills needed for achievement. Your faith and your work ethic will show that you believe that you will gain what you need later. In some cases, you are stepping out on faith during your journey because you don't have the resources, the knowledge, or the personnel, to get where you need to be. By not doing anything, you will sit in your sin. The sin of not doing what you are meant to do.

I know that I can help others through my writing and speaking. If I don't write because of a football game, a T.V. show that I want to watch, or even because I'm sleepy, I am keeping someone from reading this book. If I don't complete this book, I'm not motivating someone to go after their dreams, or teaching them how to achieve them. When I reflected back over my life, I not only had success when I worked hard and didn't procrastinate, but I also noticed doors were opened that I couldn't or didn't know how to open.

The door to securing a scholarship to a school that I'd never heard of in Montana, led me to securing my dream of playing Division I basketball.

For a coach to offer me a scholarship, sight unseen, based on a recommendation by a classmate was something I could not have orchestrated. The improvement the classmate saw in me was what I could orchestrate, however. What I orchestrated was how much I was willing to sacrifice and how hard I worked towards my goal. The input of working hard was very demanding. Looking back, I wouldn't have wanted it any other way.

Recommended Reading:

The Five People You Meet in Heaven by Mitch Albom

HUSTLE INSTRUCTIONS
REFLECTION EXPERIENCES

What Did You Learn?

_____
_____
_____
_____
_____

How Can You Apply:

_____
_____
_____
_____

What Is Your Dream?

_____
_____
_____
_____
_____
_____

What Is Your Thoughts?

_____

_____

_____

_____

_____

_____

What Did You Take Away?

_____

_____

_____

_____

_____

What Is Your Goal?

_____

_____

_____

_____

_____

_____

Notes:

_____

_____

_____

_____

_____

_____

_____

_____

_____

_____

_____

_____

_____

_____

_____

_____

_____

_____

_____

_____

_____

_____

Why Sin?

_____

_____

_____

_____

_____

_____

_____

_____

_____

_____

_____

_____

_____

_____

_____

_____

_____

_____

_____

_____

_____

_____

_____

FAITH QUOTES
Chapter 7 - Why Sin?

"We are judged by what we finish, not what we start."

- Unknown

"Always do your best, what you plant today, you will harvest later."

- Og Mandino

"Success isn't the same as talent. The world is full of incredibly talented people who never succeed at anything.

- Tim Grover

"The principle is competing against yourself. It's about self-improvement...being better than you were the day before."

- Steve Young

"To find what you seek in the road of life, the best proverb of all is that which says: 'Leave no stone unturned.'"

- Edward Bulwer Lytton

"If you have accomplished all you have planned for yourself, you have not planned enough."

- Edward Everett Hale

"When I let go of what I am, I become what I might be."

- Lao Tsu

"Although you only need the faith the size of a mustard seed in order to speak to a mountain and tell it to move, you still need the work ethic of the entire mountain in order for the mountain not to return."

- Aaron Womack, Jr.

Epilogue

I want to thank you, the reader, for allowing me to give you something to chew on and for allowing me to share my story. Yes, this book was written with the hopes of helping someone else reach their goals and dreams. As with my first book, I believe the best way for me to help you is to simply share my stories. My stories of failure, success, hopes, and dreams, not only my own, but those of the countless others I have studied. All of the stories have been used not just to motivate you, but to move you to action. I have studied successful people who are close to me and those from afar. I have a story to tell that can't be contained in the two books I have written and I look forward to reaching you with my yet to be published works. Not only do I have a story to tell but I believe every single person has a story to tell as well. I want to help you tell your story.

The best way to help you achieve is to begin to write your thoughts down. That is why the backbone of every great educator is lesson planning. Lesson plans are not just about the activities that students will experience, but they are about where a teacher wants to take their students and how they will help them get there. My first book, as well as this one, began as a lesson plan and evolved into me telling my stories.

Telling your story, I believe, will be a way for you to reach your destination. Your destination may simply bring closure to a part of your life that is holding you back.

Telling your story may help you get rid of the skeletons in your closet. Pastor Andre Atwater, from Milwaukee, Wisconsin states, "Exposure brings closure." Whether your exposure brings you to be a published author or helps you to create a manuscript that you don't want to publish but just keep for yourself, you can benefit from putting pen to paper and telling your story.

Who knows, you may find telling your story makes you focus on your goals and develops into your "Why" which you can use to help yourself. William P. Young, author of *The Shack*, didn't have the financial means to give his family gifts at Christmas, so he decided to write a letter. The letter turned into a story which turned into a book which turned into a movie. You can find many other stories like this with a search on the internet. Let your simple writing assignment turn into a novel.

I hear from many people who have come to my speaking engagements, seminars, or have read my books; they also want to write a book but don't know how to get started. Let me help you with the start.

You will find in the following pages a template taken from an educational viewpoint. You can take a step-by-step approach to writing your sentences, paragraphs, and eventually a finished product.

The template is to help you find out more about you. I believe you can't help others unless you help yourself. Part of helping yourself is knowing who you are. Being able to tell your story starts with knowing you and what you are about. The template will help you understand what has shaped you. This will become your foundation. The template helped me to finally understand I wasn't where I wanted to be achievement wise because of ME. I had no one to blame but me. I received a lower grade in school because I didn't work hard enough. Consequently, I received higher grades not because the teacher liked me, but because I busted my butt. The same worked with playing time when I played basketball.

Writing my story and getting to know myself drove me to a passion of motivating others and becoming an author. You are an author. Are you ready to get started?

Good, no rush, take your time. You may be moved to do a paragraph a month, every other week, or each week. It's up to you. If you wish to make your story into a book and need some assistances, then don't hesitate to contact me or one of my assistants as we would love to help you in the writing process.

We are available, through my company, An Hour Early, LLC, to assist as coach, co-writer, or ghost writer. The hardest part of getting started is getting started. Let the template help you get started. Once you start, you are on your way. I'll see you at the finish line.

GET YOUR HUSTLE BACK IN 90 DAYS...

Journal

Faith Journal:

_____
_____
_____
_____
_____
_____
_____
_____
_____
_____
_____
_____
_____
_____
_____
_____
_____
_____
_____
_____
_____
_____
_____
_____
_____
_____
_____
_____

Faith Journal:

_____
_____
_____
_____
_____
_____
_____
_____
_____
_____
_____
_____
_____
_____
_____
_____
_____
_____
_____
_____
_____
_____
_____
_____
_____
_____
_____
_____
_____

Faith Journal:

_____
_____
_____
_____
_____
_____
_____
_____
_____
_____
_____
_____
_____
_____
_____
_____
_____
_____
_____
_____
_____
_____
_____
_____
_____
_____
_____
_____

Faith Journal:

Faith Journal:

_____
_____
_____
_____
_____
_____
_____
_____
_____
_____
_____
_____
_____
_____
_____
_____
_____
_____
_____
_____
_____
_____
_____
_____
_____
_____
_____
_____

Faith Journal:

_____
_____
_____
_____
_____
_____
_____
_____
_____
_____
_____
_____
_____
_____
_____
_____
_____
_____
_____
_____
_____
_____
_____
_____
_____
_____
_____
_____

Faith Journal:

_____
_____
_____
_____
_____
_____
_____
_____
_____
_____
_____
_____
_____
_____
_____
_____
_____
_____
_____
_____
_____
_____
_____
_____
_____
_____
_____
_____
_____

Faith Journal:

_____
_____
_____
_____
_____
_____
_____
_____
_____
_____
_____
_____
_____
_____
_____
_____
_____
_____
_____
_____
_____
_____
_____
_____
_____
_____
_____
_____
_____

Faith Journal:

_____
_____
_____
_____
_____
_____
_____
_____
_____
_____
_____
_____
_____
_____
_____
_____
_____
_____
_____
_____
_____
_____
_____
_____
_____
_____
_____
_____

Faith Journal:

_____
_____
_____
_____
_____
_____
_____
_____
_____
_____
_____
_____
_____
_____
_____
_____
_____
_____
_____
_____
_____
_____
_____
_____
_____
_____
_____
_____
_____
_____

Faith Journal:

_____
_____
_____
_____
_____
_____
_____
_____
_____
_____
_____
_____
_____
_____
_____
_____
_____
_____
_____
_____
_____
_____
_____
_____
_____
_____
_____
_____

Faith Journal:

Faith Journal:

_____
_____
_____
_____
_____
_____
_____
_____
_____
_____
_____
_____
_____
_____
_____
_____
_____
_____
_____
_____
_____
_____
_____
_____
_____
_____
_____
_____
_____

Faith Journal:

_____

_____

_____

_____

_____

_____

_____

_____

_____

_____

_____

_____

_____

_____

_____

_____

_____

_____

_____

_____

_____

_____

_____

_____

_____

_____

_____

_____

Faith Journal:

_____
_____
_____
_____
_____
_____
_____
_____
_____
_____
_____
_____
_____
_____
_____
_____
_____
_____
_____
_____
_____
_____
_____
_____
_____
_____
_____

Faith Journal:

_____
_____
_____
_____
_____
_____
_____
_____
_____
_____
_____
_____
_____
_____
_____
_____
_____
_____
_____
_____
_____
_____
_____
_____
_____
_____
_____
_____
_____
_____
_____

Faith Journal:

_____
_____
_____
_____
_____
_____
_____
_____
_____
_____
_____
_____
_____
_____
_____
_____
_____
_____
_____
_____
_____
_____
_____
_____
_____
_____
_____
_____
_____
_____

Faith Journal:

_____
_____
_____
_____
_____
_____
_____
_____
_____
_____
_____
_____
_____
_____
_____
_____
_____
_____
_____
_____
_____
_____
_____
_____
_____
_____
_____

Faith Journal:

_____
_____
_____
_____
_____
_____
_____
_____
_____
_____
_____
_____
_____
_____
_____
_____
_____
_____
_____
_____
_____
_____
_____
_____
_____
_____
_____
_____
_____

Faith Journal:

_____
_____
_____
_____
_____
_____
_____
_____
_____
_____
_____
_____
_____
_____
_____
_____
_____
_____
_____
_____
_____
_____
_____
_____
_____
_____
_____
_____
_____
_____

Faith Journal:

_____
_____
_____
_____
_____
_____
_____
_____
_____
_____
_____
_____
_____
_____
_____
_____
_____
_____
_____
_____
_____
_____
_____
_____
_____
_____
_____
_____

Faith Journal:

_____
_____
_____
_____
_____
_____
_____
_____
_____
_____
_____
_____
_____
_____
_____
_____
_____
_____
_____
_____
_____
_____
_____
_____
_____
_____
_____
_____
_____
_____

Faith Journal:

Faith Journal:

_____
_____
_____
_____
_____
_____
_____
_____
_____
_____
_____
_____
_____
_____
_____
_____
_____
_____
_____
_____
_____
_____
_____
_____
_____
_____
_____
_____
_____
_____

Faith Journal:

_____
_____
_____
_____
_____
_____
_____
_____
_____
_____
_____
_____
_____
_____
_____
_____
_____
_____
_____
_____
_____
_____
_____
_____
_____
_____
_____
_____
_____

Faith Journal:

_____
_____
_____
_____
_____
_____
_____
_____
_____
_____
_____
_____
_____
_____
_____
_____
_____
_____
_____
_____
_____
_____
_____
_____
_____
_____
_____
_____

Faith Journal:

_____
_____
_____
_____
_____
_____
_____
_____
_____
_____
_____
_____
_____
_____
_____
_____
_____
_____
_____
_____
_____
_____
_____
_____
_____
_____
_____
_____
_____

Faith Journal:

_____
_____
_____
_____
_____
_____
_____
_____
_____
_____
_____
_____
_____
_____
_____
_____
_____
_____
_____
_____
_____
_____
_____
_____
_____
_____
_____
_____
_____
_____
_____